A NEW DEAL FOR SECRETARIES?

Other titles from IES:

Temporary Work and the Labour Market
J Atkinson, J Rick, S Morris, M Williams
IES Report 311, 1996. ISBN 1-85184-237-3

Strategies for Career Development: Promise, Practice and Pretence
W Hirsh, C Jackson
IES Report 305, 1996. ISBN 1-85184-231-4

The Skills Review Programme titles will include:
Sales Assistants; Sales and Marketing; Engineering;
Computing; Senior Managers; Process Workers; Care Workers

A catalogue of these and over 100 other titles is available from IES.

the | INSTITUTE
for | EMPLOYMENT
STUDIES

A New Deal For Secretaries?

Leslie Giles
Ivana La Valle
Sarah Perryman

REPORT 313

Published by:

THE INSTITUTE FOR EMPLOYMENT STUDIES
Mantell Building
University of Sussex
Brighton BN1 9RF
UK

Tel. + 44 (0) 1273 686751
Fax + 44 (0) 1273 690430

British Cataloguing-in-Publication Data

A catalogue record for this publication is available from the British Library

ISBN 1-85184-239-X

Printed in Great Britain by Microgen UK Ltd

The Institute for Employment Studies

IES is an independent, international centre of research and consultancy in human resource issues. It has close working contacts with employers in the manufacturing, service and public sectors, government departments, agencies, professional and employee bodies, and foundations. Since it was established 25 years ago the Institute has been a focus of knowledge and practical experience in employment and training policy, the operation of labour markets and human resource planning and development. IES is a not-for-profit organisation which has a multidisciplinary staff of over 60. IES expertise is available to all organisations through research, consultancy, training and publications.

IES aims to help bring about sustainable improvements in employment policy and human resource management. IES achieves this by increasing the understanding and improving the practice of key decision makers in policy bodies and employing organisations.

Acknowledgements

We wish to acknowledge the assistance provided by the employers, secretaries and members of various organisations who took part in the study. Many gave up valuable time to see us and their contribution was extremely valued. We would also like to thank Emma Hart, the team administrator, and Sally Dench, the project manager, for their help, support and encouragement.

Contents

Executive Summary

The Department for Education and Employment (DfEE) has commissioned the Institute for Employment Studies to conduct a study of the changing nature of skill requirements within major occupational groups in the UK. This report presents the findings on current and future skill requirements for the secretarial occupation.

The study comprised four main components: a review of available data and research literature; exploratory interviews with key players in the secretarial field; interviews with employers and secretaries in 20 organisations; and a forum where the research findings were presented and discussed with some of the research participants. The fieldwork was undertaken between autumn 1995 and spring 1996.

The place of secretaries in the sample organisations

In line with previous research we found that:

- In the majority of sample organisations the number of secretaries has declined, but in most cases the occupation has not been affected more than other groups of staff by redundancy programmes.

- The overwhelming majority of secretaries are women, most of them working full time. The use of temporary and part-time secretarial staff seems to be mainly reserved to meet short-term fluctuations in business or to provide staff cover.

- At higher levels, secretaries provide administrative support on a one-to-one basis, while at lower grades, secretaries service bigger teams of managers and professional staff.

- Salaries for secretaries vary considerably, ranging from £7,000 to £36,000.

The changing secretarial role

Our research shows that secretarial roles and functions have been changing in the past few years, and are likely to change further in the near future. The key factors driving these changes include:

- Advances in information technology and increased computerisation. These have upgraded secretarial work, as they have led to a decrease in the quantity of more routine and mundane work, and to an increase in the quality and accuracy of the work produced by secretaries.

- Changes in organisational structures. In some sample organisations the move towards flatter and less hierarchical organisational structures has given more senior secretaries the opportunity to take over some managers' responsibilities.

- Changes in organisational cultures and working practices. These have led to a shift from the 'personal' secretary working exclusively or mainly for one boss, to the team secretary providing support for a group of people.

Our findings show that in the sample organisations, the traditional secretarial role as support worker is still predominant, but has expanded considerably. Our research also points to the emergence of two new secretarial roles: namely the team player and the independent worker.

New secretarial skills

Skill requirements vary according to the nature of secretarial roles and functions in the sample organisations, the extent to which secretaries are expected to fulfil more traditional as well as new roles, and the level of seniority.

As **support workers** secretaries are expected to have good oral and written communication skills, inter-personal skills such as tact and diplomacy, and an understanding of the organisational structure and nature of the business. They also need to be able to use a range of computer applications, office equipment and technology.

As **team workers** they need to be assertive, to be able to manage pressure and conflicting demands, to have an understanding of group dynamics, be both co-operative and collaborative, and be able to manage conflict and consensus. In some organisations team secretaries are expected to provide a key link between group members, in these cases team working and co-ordination skills are regarded as essential.

As **independent workers** secretaries are developing their own areas of work and responsibilities. We identified two distinct areas where secretaries are more likely to maximise their opportunities for 'independent work', namely IT, and the broader area of secretarial training, development and supervision. In some organisations secretaries are increasingly regarded as 'IT experts', and are expected to provide formal and informal training to other staff, and to contribute to the organisation's IT policy. In some cases, more senior secretaries are also likely to get involved in secretarial recruitment, have responsibility for coaching and mentoring more junior secretarial staff, and for advising management on secretarial development and training needs.

Secretarial recruitment

Our research shows that the two most common ways of recruiting secretarial staff are via internal appointments, and secretarial agencies.

Employers do not seem to follow any 'hard and fast' rules regarding the indicators used to identify the right type and combination of secretarial skills. While employers are increasingly looking for a wider range and higher level of skills, on the whole they do not seem to have changed the indicators (*eg* educational qualifications) nor their recruitment methods, in line with their new skill needs and requirements.

Employers included in the study had not experienced any serious difficulties in finding suitably qualified and experienced secretaries, and no major skill gaps were identified. Weaker areas requiring development reflected the expansion in secretarial roles and responsibilities. These included time management, team working, assertiveness, business awareness, and knowledge of some advanced computer applications.

Secretarial training and development opportunities

Despite the current and predicted changes in the nature of secretarial work, we found little evidence that development and career opportunities for secretaries are improving significantly. Secretarial training seemed to be very *ad hoc* and rather narrow in content. The skill and training needs of the secretarial group as a whole are not generally co-ordinated or planned. Access to training largely depends on the secretary's position in the organisation, and their manager's good will and attitude towards secretarial work.

Similarly, opportunities for career development remain very limited. Secretarial career structures are very short, with very few positions available at the more senior levels. Career structures tend to be shaped around the structures and hierarchy of managerial positions. Despite the move to team secretaries, such posts are almost invariably lower down the career and hierarchical structures.

The future of the secretarial occupation

National statistical data show that the secretarial occupation has decreased in the past few years. This trend was confirmed by our research, as in virtually all sample organisations there had been a reduction in the number of secretaries employed, albeit generally only slight. However, we found little evidence that the size of the occupation will be significantly reduced in future. Our findings seem to suggest that while the number of secretarial staff has stabilised, further changes in the nature of secretarial work are likely in the future. As secretarial roles and functions become broader, secretaries will need to be even more highly competent in a broader range of technical and social skills. Rather than disappearing, as some commentators have argued, this is likely to become an occupation with higher entry requirements.

1. The Secretarial Study

1.1 Introduction

The Department for Education and Employment (DfEE) is concerned to explore in detail the changing nature of skill requirements within major occupational groups in the UK. It has commissioned the Institute for Employment Studies (IES) to undertake a programme of research entitled the Skills Review Programme. The Programme is a fairly long-running piece of research which is due to be completed in 1997. The main intention of the research is to improve the Department's knowledge of selected skills, training and occupational issues and, by so doing, to keep the government abreast of changes in the supply of, and demand for, skills at a wide range of occupational levels. The research is planned to cover eight key occupations.

This report presents the findings of one of the first occupational studies. This has examined employers' skills requirements and changes in skills for the secretarial occupation.

1.2 Aims and objectives

The research for all occupations intends to confront a number of common research questions in relation to each occupational study. These include:

- What are the nature of skill requirements for the occupation?

- Have the nature and level of skill requirements changed? Are the skill requirements increasing or decreasing? Are some 'new' skills emerging and some 'older' skills disappearing?

- Which sorts of skill requirements are increasing and which are decreasing? Which are emerging and which disappearing, if any?

- Has the skills level of the workforce changed to accommodate these changes? Or, have there been improvements in the supply of skills that have encouraged increasing skill requirements in jobs?

- Are the requirements for occupations likely to carry on increasing or decreasing? Do employers view the changes as a continuing trend?

- How can the changes in skill requirements within the occupation be measured?

The occupational standards were reviewed (together with other relevant literature and data) as part of the preliminary stage of the research, in order to develop a framework for the fieldwork. However, it must be emphasised that the study should not be viewed as an attempt to validate the occupational standards. The overall aim of the research is limited to the exploration of changes in skill requirements in the secretarial occupation. There was no attempt to establish the extent to which these changes might be reflected in the occupational standards.

The remainder of this chapter sets out the details of the research design adopted for the study of secretaries. The fieldwork was primarily comprised of two key stages: a preliminary stage of exploratory interviews, followed by a principal stage of employer interviews.

1.3 Research methodology

1.3.1 Exploratory interviews

Before progressing with the main fieldwork for the study, some preparatory fieldwork was undertaken as a preliminary stage to the research project. This involved meeting with key contacts within the secretarial field and holding a number of exploratory interviews. These contacts included:

- a DfEE representative, responsible for this occupational area

- the Administration Lead Body (ALB), responsible for developing occupational standards for all administrative workers including secretaries

- the Institute of Qualified Private Secretaries, which is a key professional organisation within the secretarial field

- organisations which represent the interests, views and concerns of secretarial workers, have a keen interest in secretaries, or have undertaken research on the secretarial profession.

These exploratory interviews were conducted to fulfil a number of objectives:

1. As key actors within the secretarial field, it was felt they may provide useful information to guide the principal part of the study, and would assist in the development of a preparatory framework for analysing employers' skill requirements. This in turn was intended to guide the course of the discussion about skills in the subsequent interviews with employers.

2. To explore the contacts' involvement in the development of the occupational standards for secretaries, and to probe their views not only about the standards and associated NVQs/SVQs, but any trends or significant developments within the occupation.

3. To inform them about the study and to gain their interest, general views and support.

4. To identify what research they have, are aware of, or are planning to undertake about the occupational group.

5. To increase our own understanding and familiarity with the occupational area, its key skills and relevant occupational standards.

The exploratory interviews were conducted in Autumn 1995. Information from these exploratory interviews was supplemented with research evidence collected from a literature review of the occupation. Both these sources of information were employed to develop the preparatory framework for looking at employers' skill requirements and the employers' interview discussion guide.

1.3.2 Employers' interviews

The principal stage of the research involved holding interviews with a number of employers. A total of 20 employer interviews was conducted in this stage of the study. Attempts were made as far as possible to ensure that interviews were conducted with the most appropriate respondent within each organisation. In most cases, this was the personnel or training manager, based at head office. These managers were usually responsible for the recruitment and/or development of secretarial workers and had knowledge of the skills and utilisation of secretaries in their respective organisations. Most interviews lasted about one and a half to two hours. In some cases, where secretaries attended the interview, it was also possible to probe their views and perceptions about trends and developments within the occupation.

Discussion guide

A common discussion guide, which had been developed for all the occupations in the skills review study, was adopted in the analysis of the secretarial occupation. The guide was piloted in the first two interviews but few modifications were deemed necessary. The discussion guide covered a number of areas. These included:

- the specific skills required of secretaries and their main functions
- how these skills are obtained:
    - external recruitment, *eg* What do they look for? How do they test for the existence of these skills or the potential for development?
    - training and development
    - internal assessment, movement and progression and the relationship to neighbouring occupations.
- how employers talk about, identify and measure skill
- how skills are changing, *ie* whether skills are increasing or decreasing, or new skills are emerging and older skills disappearing — related to changes in the organisation, in working practices, structure and organisation, technology, *etc.*
- difficulties in obtaining the skills required (internal and external skills gaps)
- future expectations: skill requirements, changes and difficulties.

The employer interviews were conducted over two months, from December 1995 to January 1996. All research participants were invited to take part in a forum where the research findings were presented and discussed. Suggestions and comments from the forum were included in the final report.

1.3.3 Sample characteristics

Employers included in the study were selected to represent a wide range of employers, and hence were intended to encompass a broad cross-section of secretaries and approaches to secretarial work. Although the study was intended to be exploratory and indicative, rather than entirely representative, it is hoped the inclusion of a wide range of organisations has gone some way to capturing the diversity of employer experiences.

Selected organisations were from both the private and public sector. The former included local authorities, hospitals, the civil service, and an educational institution. The private sector sample comprised of employers primarily from production and manufacturing industries, the financial services, retailing, and the privatised utilities. A secretarial employment agency was also included in the sample. Participating organisations varied greatly in size and most employed between several hundred to several thousand employees. Although some of the organisations were multi-national, they were all UK owned with their head office and most of their operations based in Britain. Indeed, the findings relating to the utilisation, skills and organisation of secretaries apply entirely to experiences in Britain.

A certain amount of background information was collected from each participating organisation to set a context for employers' responses. Such information provided a vital insight into the structure, culture and development of organisations. This assisted, in particular, in the overall understanding and analysis of the skill requirements of secretaries, and how they are changing. A number of common and interesting organisational developments and changes were identified.

1.3.4 Recent changes in the sample organisations

All sample employers had experienced organisational change in the past few years. This is undoubtedly due in part to changes in the broader socio-economic, political and legal climate during the 1980s and 1990s, which have given rise to a number of developments generally in the world of work. The changes experienced within the participating organisations, therefore, appear to be in line with developments observed more broadly in public and private sector organisations, and outlined extensively in the literature.

These broad observations show that in a period of heightened competition and significant changes in world trading patterns, organisations in general have been forced to review their working practices and to seek ways of operating more effectively.

A wide range of organisational responses have been implemented in the name of survival and in the pursuit of reduced cost, increased organisational productivity, performance and profitability. These include:

- reorganising working practices and implementing major redundancy and streamlining programmes, particularly in labour intensive areas such as administration and middle management

- restructuring the organisation internally and decentralising accountability and management control to divisional business units, and by so doing allowing managers greater discretion locally, albeit within centrally determined guidelines and frameworks

- moving away from hierarchical organisational structures towards flatter, more dynamic structures, which can respond more quickly to changes in the market place

- implementing more flexible forms of working, such as part-time and fixed-term employment, which can fit more closely with organisational operations and variations in business activity

- introducing various forms of new technology to reduce labour costs in some areas and to increase efficiency and productivity

- increasing the use of sub-contracting in more peripheral areas of the organisation so that resources can be concentrated on core business activities.

Many senior executives in both private and public organisations, have launched these changes within a number of wide ranging change management programmes. These have aimed at:

- establishing new corporate cultures

- enhancing 'total quality' of goods and services by fostering values such as greater customer orientation, customer sovereignty and customer care, individualism, enterprise, innovation, initiative, flexibility and competitiveness.

- developing a quality workforce by implementing more innovative employment practices, emphasising employee commitment, empowerment, higher individual performance, flexibility and task interchangeability, teamwork, training and development.

Such developments have been observed, albeit to varying degrees, in all the participating organisations and provide an important backdrop to the study of secretarial workers.

1.4 Report outline

The next chapter sets a framework for the investigation by discussing the findings from the review of relevant data and literature, and by exploring trends in the size and composition of the secretarial occupation. Chapter 3 presents some of the general, contextual information in relation to the place of secretaries in the sample organisations. Chapter 4 discusses the research findings in relation to changes in secretarial roles and the implications for skill requirements. Chapter 5 looks at the ways in which participating employers identified and measured the skills required for secretarial work, and to what extent the supply of skills matched their requirements. Chapter 6 explores opportunities for development and training for secretaries, and the factors impinging negatively on the efforts to improve their position in the sample organisations. In the finally chapter, some examples of good practice are presented, and then conclusions are drawn from our findings on the future of the secretarial occupation.

2. The Secretarial Occupation

2.1 Introduction

Clerical and secretarial work are thought to be similar in many respects, particularly in relation to the physical working environment, the machinery and materials used, and the change processes they have experienced or been subjected to within their working environment. As a consequence their working practices have often been studied together (*eg* Lane, 1989). Indeed, the Skills and Enterprise Briefing (1992) stated that clerical and secretarial skills are easily transferable. Research has identified many skills common to these occupations. These include oral and written communication, handling and using information, dealing with detail and accuracy, an organised approach, team orientation, planning and analysing, dealing with customers, initiative and flexibility (Gilligan, 1995; Anderson and Marshall, 1994; IDS, 1994; Pringle, 1989; Webster, 1986). With the introduction of new technology and the incorporation of word-processing it may be increasingly more difficult to discern clear and distinct occupational boundaries within the office. This chapter attempts to explore, within the literature, some of the main skills and functions of secretaries in more detail, and the size and basic composition of the secretarial occupation. This may provide a fuller insight into the occupation and may also serve to clarify where occupational differences and boundaries might lie.

2.2 What is a secretary?

Secretarial work is characterised by very particular tasks (Webster, 1986). Their primary role is usually to provide a support and administrative service to a manager, a group of managers or professional staff. Past studies have identified four elements of secretarial work. These include:

- gatekeeping, such as dealing with visitors, the post and telephone calls

- text production, including typing and word-processing

- routine office work, such as filing, photocopying and sending faxes

- working on one's own initiative, involving general administration and conference organisation (Truss, 1993).

Secretaries have, thus, been observed to combine a number of mechanical tasks with more social tasks (Lane, 1989; Webster, 1986). The mechanical element of the job would include things such as typing, filing, audio and shorthand, and the social side would involve the general administrative tasks, dealing with clients and visitors, either face to face or through telephone calls, and providing a service to their manager or managers. This latter element of providing a support service to the boss, combined with the fact that most secretaries are women, has led to some researchers referring to secretaries as the 'office wife'. Webster (1986) reports that 'office wives' are often expected to anticipate their bosses' every requirement, to shield their managers from unwelcome callers and to provide emotional and psychological support. According to Pringle (1989) the two main requirements of such a connotation is that the secretary must be deferential and ladylike. In addition, she is also often assumed to be loyal, trustworthy and devoted to her boss.

The traditional or classical secretarial role is considered to be quite narrow in focus, only involving typing, telephone calls, post, diary and filing (Truss, 1993), and in the past, most secretaries would have tended to serve one manager. However, as roles have developed in line with organisational changes, secretaries have acquired more varied administrative tasks, and they have increasingly worked for more than one person (Skills and Enterprise Briefing, 1992). The exception perhaps to this narrow, traditional role may have been at the most senior secretarial level of personal assistant (PA), who usually works for the most senior chairperson or chief executive of an organisation. As seniority has increased, the secretarial role has generally been seen to have had more responsibility, authority, to involve more discretion, and also has often demanded a broader range of skills. As well as needing the more traditional skills such as office management and communication, these PA roles appear to have also emphasised things such as diplomacy, judgement and proactivity (Gilligan, 1995).

The status of secretaries has generally been closely linked with that of their boss, and their career structures have usually been short. The most common have extended from typists and junior secretaries, often undertaking a very narrow range of tasks perhaps within a typing pool, through middle and senior secretarial levels, to the most senior secretaries in the form of the PA. Secretaries' opportunities to advance have generally relied on the development of their boss rather than there being a clearly defined career structure in most organisations (Truss, 1993; Skills and Enterprise Briefing, 1992; Industrial Society, 1990). Indeed, individual progression has mainly been reserved for the particularly career-minded and opportunistic secretaries (Truss, 1993).

Although some secretaries may have a narrow range of tasks, with most of their time consumed by routine office work, the pattern of secretarial work has generally allowed secretaries significant control over their work. Indeed, Truss (1993) found that even more traditional secretaries had considerable scope over the order in which they carried out tasks and the form the work took. In addition, Webster (1986) has stated that most secretaries have a reasonable amount of autonomy to decide how to organise job tasks and regulate their own pace of work in accordance with how much time they have to spend on it. Vinnicombe (1980) states, in support of this, that secretaries organise their own work around what they consider to be the most efficient lines.

Clerical work in general appears to deviate from secretarial work in several ways. Clerical work is generally of a lower status than secretarial work (Skills and Enterprise Briefing, 1992). Furthermore, a clerk's work is often characterised by functional specialisation (Lane, 1989) and hence will be more functionally based. This frequently means clerical jobs have been reduced to similar singular tasks or groups of simple tasks which are highly specialised, often routinised, standardised, controlled through set procedures and systems, and focused on a specific function. The job may thus require limited skills and offer little discretion and responsibility. In banking and the financial services, such tasks may include cashiering, routine money services and handling, remittance work, data processing, inputting and coding, and a range of office tasks like filing and photocopying. In some cases a clerk's job may also involve functions such as customer enquiries, liaison with brokers, processing of new applications, underwriting within set limits and claims handling. Clerical workers may also be less likely to have a clearly defined career structure, with the most mundane clerical jobs having particularly limited career prospects (Lane, 1989). As a consequence, particularly ambitious clerks appear usually to have pursued a more functional route through, for example, the banking profession, rather than staying in a more general administrative route (Lane, 1989).

2.3 The size of the secretarial occupation

As indicated in Figure 2.1, clerical and secretarial employment grew steadily from the beginning of the century up to the early 1980s, when the proportion of the workforce employed in these occupations started to decline.

2.3.1 Trends through the last century

There was a dramatic increase in the extent of secretarial and clerical related employment from the latter part of last century up to the early 1980s. Crompton and Jones (1984) report that in 1851, clerical staff comprised less than one per cent of the workforce. By 1901 this had risen to four per cent, by 1951 it was nearly 11 per cent, in 1971 the corresponding figure was 11 per cent, and by 1981 secretarial and clerical related staff made up 18 per cent of the entire workforce. The continuing growth in the service sector through the 20th century undoubtedly has been a significant feature in this general growth.

2.3.2 Current occupational size

After reaching a peak in 1981, secretarial and clerical employment began to decline. Skills and Enterprise Network (1995) estimated that in 1994 secretarial and clerical occupations comprised 14 per cent of the worforce. Data from the Labour Force Survey (LFS, 1995) provides more specific and up-to-date figures. According to the LFS statistics, in 1995 there were 854,400 secretaries which comprised 3.1 per cent of the entire UK workforce. This figure included 628,500 individuals who were solely secretaries and 225,900 receptionists and reception telephonists. In addition, there were some 2,190,000 clerical workers making up almost eight per cent of the UK workforce. These consisted of approximately 340,100 administrative staff in government, and some 1,849,900 numerical clerks and cashiers including accounts clerks, counter clerks, filing and record clerks, and book-keepers.

Figure 2.1: Proportion of workforce in secretarial and clerical occupations 1901-2001

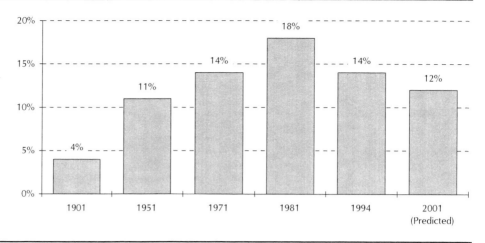

Source: Crompton and Jones (1984), Skills and Enterprise Network (1995)

2.3.3 Future trends

It is currently uncertain how secretarial employment will fare in the future. Some have predicted that with the broad changes in business activity, organisational structures, working practices and the growing emphasis on cost efficiency and competition, secretarial and clerical employment may suffer and reduce at the expense of the more valued operational, professional, technical and functional types of employment. In addition, many have expected clerical and secretarial occupations to have been detrimentally affected by the widespread introduction of new technology and office automation such as word-processors, 'smart' copiers with microelectronic 'intelligence', computers, electronic mail facilities and computer network systems.

It is argued by some that technology may lead to deskilling, routinisation of tasks, intensification of workloads, and in severe cases may affect overall levels of secretarial and clerical employment (Morgall, 1986; Crompton and Jones, 1984; Glen and Feldberg, 1982). Indeed, early forecasts, assessing the impact of new technology, ranged from modest job losses (Sleigh, 1979) to predictions that as many as 40 per cent of clerical and related jobs would be threatened in the future (Virgo, 1979). More recently the Skills and Enterprise Network (1995) has supported a more modest decline, predicting a two per cent fall in numbers by the year 2001. However, with the rapid changes in UK industry, the continual expansion in the service sector, and

The Institute for Employment Studies

variation in employment levels generally, such predictions are difficult to make with any certainty. The clerical and secretarial occupations still remain a significant component of the UK workforce.

2.4 The composition of the secretarial occupation

Through the last century there have also been quite significant changes in the composition of secretarial and clerical related work. While clerical work was largely a male preserve in the late 19th century, research has shown that it has become a leading female occupation in the 20th century (*eg* Lowe, 1987). Indeed, Crompton and Jones (1984) note that, although in 1851 few women held clerical positions, by 1901 over 13 per cent of clerks were women and this had risen to nearly 60 per cent by 1951. Research in Australia (Pringle, 1989) has identified similar trends amongst secretarial and clerical related work. Thus, for example, whereas in the late 19th century the majority of secretaries were male, by the 1950s a male secretary was said to be rare. Several studies, in particular, have identified secretarial work as a highly 'feminised' occupation. These were conducted in a range of countries, including the UK, France, Germany and America (*eg* Truss, 1993).

Some researchers have attempted to explore the reasons for this transition in the composition of clerical and secretarial work. In Britain, in particular, it appears that the 'feminisation' of these occupations was primarily assisted by the expansion of such work, associated with the boom in trade and commerce in the 19th century, and the introduction of typewriters, during the 1880s, which were said to favour female dexterity. At the same time there were also generally more women in paid employment, and women with higher levels of education were deterred from other areas, such as retailing and domestic work, by low rates of pay (Lowe, 1987).

The domination of the occupation by women has continued through the latter part of the 20th century. According to the Skills and Enterprise Briefing, in 1992, women comprised 87 per cent of clerical workers and 97 per cent of secretaries. The most recent figures from the Skills and Enterprise Network (1995) show that 71 per cent of clerical workers and 97 per cent of secretaries are women. Predictions for the next five years show little change in the gender composition of the occupation.

The Skills and Enterprise Briefing (1992) also shows that women in clerical and secretarial work generally have low or no qualifications. This has been supported by the work of Truss (1993) and is believed to be partly a function of the broad range of possible qualifications available in Britain, and the number of different examining boards and accrediting bodies. Indeed, in 1990 the Industrial Society estimated that there were 297 different vocational secretarial qualifications offered by 11 examining boards at five different levels (Industrial Society, 1990). In her study of 400 secretaries in England, France and Germany, Truss found that in England the majority of secretaries had pursued formal education just until the school leaving age. Fifty-nine per cent had 'O' levels or below, 31 per cent had 'A' levels, and just under ten per cent had a degree. Sixty-six per cent of secretaries had attended a specific secretarial course, but the single most common qualification was typing: 89 per cent of English secretaries included in the study had a typing qualification (Truss, 1994).

Truss also found that such secretarial training as was available was narrow in focus, appeared confined to purely secretarial skills in typing and audio or shorthand, and tended not to include broader academic subjects, as was the case in France. She suggested that this narrow focus of training was a function of the generally narrow focus of secretarial work at that time, particularly in comparison to secretarial work in other European countries studied.

The Institute for Employment Studies

3. The Place of Secretaries in Organisations

3.1 Introduction

In the process of identifying the skill requirements of secretaries in this study, employers in the sample were asked general, contextual questions about this occupational group in their respective organisations. This information, as well as providing some background to the study, also enabled an insight into the varying nature, content and experiences of secretaries from a number of different industries, sectors and organisations. The main areas explored and presented in this chapter include:

- what is a secretary? This explores the deployment of secretaries, and the relationship between secretaries and neighbouring occupations in the sample organisations
- the number and breakdown of secretaries
- the age profile of secretaries
- the location of secretaries, and
- the salary levels and working arrangements of this occupational group.

3.2 What is a secretary in the sample organisations?

A more complete insight into what the secretarial function encompasses, within the respective organisations, was obtained by identifying the general role of secretaries, and then by examining their relationship to similar occupations.

3.2.1 The deployment of secretaries

The secretaries within the sample organisations generally provide an administrative support service to managers and professional staff. At higher levels in the organisation, such as chief executive, director or senior management levels, this is on a one-to-one basis. Secretaries at this level are generally directly responsible to their manager, and this has often appeared to foster very close working relationships and team work, with the secretary and manager often developing their own, personalised procedures, systems of working, informal practices and standards.

However, at lower levels these close working relationships between a single manager and secretary are generally being diluted, as a growing number of lower grade secretaries are servicing bigger teams of managers and professional staff or whole departments. Many of these lower level secretaries increasingly have less time now to devote to one individual. The numbers of managers served depends on the level of the secretary, with lower grade secretaries generally serving bigger teams or departments. These usually vary from four managers to as many as 25 or 30. Where typists and word processor operators are identified in the career structure, these individuals are likely to be undertaking editing and text production and, as one respondent called it, the 'overload' of copy typing for department staff. This is frequently undertaken within a typing pool, comprising of several typists or word processor operators.

3.2.2 Relationship to other neighbouring occupations

The literature has demonstrated the ambiguities associated with clearly defining the secretarial function (see Chapter 2). This has primarily been due to the great similarities in office based work, office functions, and between the tasks of secretaries and other clerical and administrative workers. In association with these observations, our research did identify some ambiguity between these 'neighbouring' occupational groups. Indeed, the boundaries between different grades of secretaries and other clerical and administrative workers do not always appear in practice to be completely clear cut. This can have important implications for the secretarial function, since secretaries and their neighbouring occupations frequently appear to be located within separate career structures, and therefore often have different job grades, terms and conditions, and career prospects.

Many organisations which have identified separate levels of secretaries have also recognised what they regard as 'other' categories of administrative or clerical staff. These are not considered to be secretarial, although they may have included some secretarial and general office based functions like filing, sorting and distributing post, photocopying and word-processing work. These more general office workers are commonly given job titles such as: clerks, administrators, clerical workers, financial and technical clerks, and marketing, production and personnel assistants. In many cases they are more junior jobs, and consist of a rather narrow range of more menial or specialised functions. These jobs are generally, although not exclusively, located within a separate career structure, and often are based at the lower end of professional and functional routes. For example, a personnel assistant is generally graded near the lower end of the personnel career structure.

However, ambiguities appear to arise in identifying the differences between these similar clerical related occupations. For instance, some individuals identified as purely secretarial workers, and who are located within the secretarial career structure, have 'administrator' or 'clerk' in their job title, when there are also separate clerks identified elsewhere within the organisation, who are not considered to be secretaries. It was necessary to explore the way in which such occupational differences have been identified.

A number of factors are said to distinguish these 'other' workers from a secretary. These include:

- performing a 'distinct job' in its own right
- the job content
- the job tasks and responsibilities
- the personal characteristics and skills required to undertake the job.

All or some of these factors are usually used by employers in combination, to distinguish between the different categories of workers.

Performing a distinct job in its own right appears to be one of the most important factors mentioned by managers. This relates to the fact that as secretaries serve a manager or team, and as such undertake work mainly defined and set by that manager or team, they in a sense are not considered to be undertaking a distinct job in its own right. The job is always seen to be attached to those it supports, and most (if not all) tasks of a secretary are related to the manager's job. So, for instance, if a manager writes a report for a conference, a secretary will be given tasks in relation to this. They may type and present the report, retrieve and collate information for the report, organise the booking arrangements for the conference, make travel arrangements, prepare slides for the manager's presentation, and so on. The attachment of the secretarial role to that of their manager is thought to be reflected most in the fact that the secretary's grade and status generally mirror that of their manager, rather than the secretarial job in its own right.

In contrast to this situation, administrators' and clerks' jobs are considered to be more separate and distinct by employers and stand alone. Their grade and status tends to be defined in terms of the tasks they undertake, the responsibilities and content of the job, and the level of skills and experience required — and not the grade or status of their line manager. However, with any changes in the nature and organisation of secretarial work, it is felt that this distinction may be increasingly more difficult to discern. This is especially the case for those secretaries who may begin working within teams or for more than one manager, and assume progressively more responsibility for their own work.

The job content, tasks and responsibilities of secretaries in comparison to administrators are also important. Secretaries, often because they serve somebody else, tend to undertake functions and tasks, which are not part, or are only a small part, of an administrator's job. These include things such as diary management, gatekeeping and dealing with telephone and general enquiries, entertaining of guests or organising meetings, travel arrangements or conferences. They are also often thought to require or employ skills not strictly stipulated for administrative work, such as shorthand, fast typing speeds, and experience of audio typing, for example. Some employers, in particular, appear to use the amount of typing as one indicator, and state, for example, that if an individual is typing for more than 50 per cent of their time, they are more likely to be involved in secretarial work. However, workloads are changeable, and tasks may continually vary in response to changes in the manager's workload or job content and/or broad changes in the organisation. It is felt in practice that this type of indicator may be problematic to implement for gauging differences between occupations.

Similarly, there may be areas within an administrator's job not usually encompassed in secretarial work. This is usually stated to be related to the level of functional knowledge required by the job holder. In line with the literature delineated in the earlier chapter (namely, Lane, 1989), it was found, amongst the sample organisations, that the work of administrators and related clerical staff is often more specialised and/or functional than secretaries. Employers stated that although administrators may undertake some so called secretarial tasks, such as word processing and typing, these do not generally constitute the only part or most significant part of the job. A greater depth of functional and specialist knowledge relating to the department in which they work is also often required. Thus a personnel assistant, for example, will be quite knowledgeable about the personnel function and may even specialise within a particular area such as payroll. Secretaries' roles overall tend thus to be more generalised. It is generally the case that as soon as a job begins to incorporate more functional and specialist knowledge, this warrants a regrading to a more specialised and functional job title. However, this implies that jobs have to be regularly reviewed and updated to gauge and keep abreast of these types of change. If changes in job content are quite frequent or the degree of specialisation is variable, it might in practice prove to be more problematic detecting subtle changes from broad based secretarial work to more specialised administrative work and vice-versa. Detecting the point at which a secretary becomes an administrator can therefore appear to be quite subjective, often relying on personal judgements about different job types and functions.

3.3 Numbers and breakdown of secretaries

The interviews with the sample employers assessed the skill requirements and changes within approximately 4,000 to 5,000 secretarial jobs. It is not possible to enter a detailed quantitative analysis of the size and composition of secretaries. Only a small number of employers was studied, and the data they could supply was incomplete; statistical breakdowns of their workforce were only approximate. However, employers perceptions of changes in the composition and size were explored qualitatively in more detail.

All employers reported that the number of secretaries had either fallen or stayed the same over the past few years. Any reductions in the numbers are primarily due to natural wastage and a result of the fact that employers are not automatically replacing secretaries who leave. There is a growing tendency for organisations, when somebody leaves, to review their job very carefully and to establish whether it is necessary to replace them. Indeed, some organisations have introduced a complete block on the recruitment of secretarial staff. Any increases in the workload are commonly redistributed amongst the workforce with existing staff expected to take up the extra load. This in many cases is thought to have led to a general intensification in work not only amongst secretaries but other office based staff. Even when business activity increases, managers appear to hold off recruitment processes for as long as they can until the work burdens became too great for existing staff to bear. Although some secretaries have been offered voluntary redundancy packages this is not very common.

In line with observations in the literature discussed in Chapter 2, our study found that in most organisations all secretaries were female. More recently some men were reported as having applied for secretarial posts, but the applicants were not suitably qualified so this had generally not altered the compositions of the occupation. Overall, respondents believed that men are not attracted to this type of work. A proportion of men appeared to enter more general administrative roles, particularly where there were opportunities to progress into professional positions.

The majority of secretaries in the sample organisations, usually amounting to at least 90 per cent, worked full time and there are generally few temporary workers. These generally appear to constitute only a small percentage of the secretarial workforce at any one time. Indeed, with the recent emphasis on cost efficiency, the use of temporary staff appeared to be reserved more for particularly busy periods, to meet short-term fluctuations in business, and to provide cover for sickness and some maternity leave. It was thus not commonly a long-term solution to staffing problems. Generally, as already stated, employers appear to expect the existing workforce to cope with any increases in workloads as far as possible. The use of temporary workers is more likely where a block has been placed on recruitment leaving less opportunity to recruit more staff to relieve the load.

The use of part-time workers is also not very common. This type of contract generally appears to be offered more frequently to women who have finished maternity leave and are hoping to return to work, or those who are about to go on maternity leave. A few organisations have job share schemes in place, but again these are generally very limited in number.

3.4 The age profile

The ages of secretaries range from 16 to 50, the most common age band being 20 to 50. Most employers generally do not try to target particular age groups. The exception is the 16 to 18 age group. In this age band a few organisations are fostering links with local colleges and operating a form of secretarial youth training scheme, to encourage younger secretaries to enter the organisation at a lower secretarial level. The intention is to develop secretaries internally for the future. However, such options tend to be limited in the organisations studied, and one organisation had recently had to disband such a scheme to conserve costs.

Senior secretaries are usually older and more junior secretaries normally younger, since seniority generally reflects experience. Some organisations stated that they feel the age profile of secretaries seems to be becoming younger, with a greater concentration of staff aged in their 20s. However, they did not have any evidence to substantiate this, and are generally unsure of the reasons for it. They perceived that it may partly be a function of the rapid changes in the organisation and the occupation, and also due to the introduction and continual development of new technology.

3.5 The location of secretaries

Secretarial workers are found throughout the organisation, from central locations at head office to more local regional, divisional and individual branch and business unit level. In addition, they are found to be servicing managers in a wide range of functions, including personnel, production, marketing, finance, operations and so on. Although they are not restricted to any one particular location, function or department, they do often appear to be more concentrated at the centre of many organisations, namely at head office or regional centres. This undoubtedly mirrors the distribution of managers in the organisation and the fact that there is a higher concentration of more senior managers and directors centrally. In some organisations this distribution seems to be a reflection of restructuring processes. Blocks on recruitment, and restrictions on replacing individuals who leave, appear to be more strictly applied in peripheral areas of the business. The more essential and important functions still often seem to be supported by a secretarial function. Indeed, at the most senior levels this is still on a one-to-one basis.

3.6 Salary levels and working arrangements

Salaries for secretaries generally range from around £7,000 for the most junior typist roles in the lowest grades, to approximately £36,000 for some of the most senior PA roles. However, not all organisations were able to stipulate a salary level and some could only provide approximations of the actual salary levels of secretaries in their organisation.

Table 3.1 shows the size distribution of salaries reported at the upper and lower end of each organisation's secretarial scale. Most of the lower salaries reported are found to be below £10,000 and most of the salaries at the upper end of the secretarial salary scale appear to be between £16,000 and £20,000. The average of the lowest salaries given is £10,700 and the average upper salary is £22,200. In general, private sector secretaries earn more than those in the public sector. Salaries quoted for the private sector range from about £9,000 to £36,000 and the average salary range is found to be between £11,400 and £22,800. In contrast, in the public sector, reported salaries range from £7,000 to £26,000 and the average salary based on the quoted figures ranges from £7,100 to £16,000.

Table 3.1: Size distribution of upper and lower secretarial salaries

Salary ranges (£)	No. of organisations with their lowest secretarial salary in this range	No. of organisations with their upper secretarial salary in this range
10,000 and below	8	—
11,000-15,000	6	1
16,000-20,000	1	9
21,000-25,000	—	2
26,000 and above	—	3

Five organisations did not provide salary details

Source: IES Secretarial Study, 1996

Generally speaking, PAs and personal secretaries are found in the better paid positions, with their status and pay closely linked to the position and status of their manager. On the other hand, secretaries servicing teams of managers and professional staff tend to earn less, as they are in lower level positions (see Chapter 6 for a full discussion of career structures).

Full-time secretaries' contractual hours range from 35 to 40 hours a week and the majority appear to be employed for 37 hours a week. Part-timers are employed for a variable number of hours, ranging from a minimum of 12 to a maximum of 30 hours a week. The number of hours are chosen to satisfy both the organisation's, the manager's, and the individual secretary's needs. However, most employers feel that the number of hours worked, whether full time or part time, fluctuate from week to week. In general, the weekly contractual hours are thought to be an underestimation of the secretary's time and thus the majority are probably working longer hours. There generally appears, however, to be an expectation that secretaries must be quite flexible about the amount of time they work, and this should be adapted to meet the manager's workload requirements. Some employers believe that managers and secretaries often develop their own informal working practices. Thus, if a manager is particularly busy a secretary is expected to stay late, but in contrast, at less busy times, some secretaries may be allowed to leave earlier or take time off 'unofficially' in lieu.

Most secretaries are not employed on flexi-time and overtime, where it is paid, is only available to lower paid staff and is generally monitored very closely by managers and kept to a minimum limit. If too much overtime is claimed, this often initiates a review of the working system and secretarial workloads. In some cases overtime is only paid for after the first full hour of work. In other cases employers report that secretaries enjoy their work so much they often do not claim for overtime pay at all!

4. Secretarial Skills

4.1 Introduction

As discussed earlier, there is much ambiguity about what constitutes a secretary's work as, unlike most other occupations, secretaries have tended to be described in terms of what they are (*eg* 'office wives', 'blonde dolly birds', deferential, ladylike and an extension of their boss), rather than what they do. Pringle has described secretaries as a 'fluid and shifting category' (Pringle, 1993, p.134). While her research focused mainly on a sociological definition of the occupation, a similar observation would apply when exploring skill requirements in secretarial employment.

From the interview data, considerable variations emerged in terms of job descriptions, skill requirements and levels, and criteria for selection and promotion. In some organisations a secretary's job description consisted of a very general and brief statement (perhaps as short as a paragraph) of the main tasks and duties, with little or no distinction between competences required at different levels. This lack of attention to job descriptions appears to show some similarity with earlier findings from the Industrial Society (1990), which found that one third of secretaries in its study had no job description at all. This did not, however, appear to apply to everyone. Indeed, a few organisations in our study had very detailed job descriptions, with clearly defined tasks, responsibilities and core competences for secretaries at different levels.

Variations in relation to the minimum skills secretaries were expected to have were closely linked to the position of this group within the organisation, and more specifically the extent to which an employer had recently reviewed and redefined secretarial roles and functions. We found considerable differences between employers in terms of how far they had gone (or they intended to go) in restructuring the occupation and its role within the organisation. However, it must be emphasised that while some organisations had more vision than others in terms of defining the secretarial role, there was usually a considerable gap between rhetoric and reality. Indeed, even the more advanced organisations we contacted, still tended to be in the early stages of implementing and achieving their vision.

Three key themes emerged from our research in relation to skill requirements in the occupation. Firstly, our findings show that many traditional secretarial skills remain important, but the level at which these skills are required has increased considerably. Secondly, while there is some evidence that some traditional secretarial skills are becoming less important, our findings are not conclusive. The extent to which these skills are and will remain important and relevant in the future, is a matter for debate among experts in this field. Finally, new skill areas were identified. In some organisations, secretaries are already expected to possess some of these 'new' skills, while in others these are more likely to represent future skill requirements and areas for further development. It must be emphasised however, that the distinction between traditional /current skill requirements on the one hand, and new/future skill requirements, on the other, is not as clear cut as our classification suggests. Some of the 'new' skills identified by some organisations as future skill require-ments, were already expected by other employers. Similarly, some traditional secretarial skills (particularly those linked to text production) have evolved to such an extent that they could hardly be described as 'traditional'.

These themes are explored and developed in this chapter. The discussion on current and future skill requirements is preceded by a section which explores changes in the secretarial role and functions. This provides important contextual information and sets a framework for the analysis of changing skill requirements in the occupation.

4.2 Changes in the secretarial role

As discussed earlier, in the past decade changes in the wider labour market, and in particular the drive towards increased efficiency, have forced employers to seriously re-think their business strategies and working practices. Our findings show that as part of this 'cultural revolution' some organisations have begun to give thought to what in the past has often been a forgotten and invisible occupational group.

Advances in information technology (IT) and increased computerisation, changes in organisational cultures and structures, and the emergence of new management and organisation theories, have greatly influenced moves towards a redefinition of the secretarial role and skill requirements. As mentioned earlier, the extent to which the latter might have changed varied considerably, and often there was a significant gap between theory and practice. However, the inevitability of change was recognised by most (if not all) research participants. It was widely accepted that secretarial roles will have to expand (further) to accommodate rapid organisational change and business needs.

4.2.1 Information technology

The advent of new technology and increased computerisation are probably the factors which have had the greatest impact on skill requirements in the occupation. Despite some debate about the effect of IT on secretarial work (*eg* Skills and Enterprise Network, 1992; Fearfull, 1992; Morgall, 1986), there can be no doubt that it has upgraded the job. Our findings show that IT has influenced work content in two ways: firstly, it has resulted in a decrease in routine work; and secondly, it has increased the quality and accuracy of the work produced by secretaries.

We found that in the sample organisations, IT has considerably reduced the quantity of more routine and mundane work (*eg* typing and re-typing) because many routine tasks have been eliminated (*eg* layout of many standard documents is already on file). But more crucially, because an increasing number of managers and professional staff have direct access to office based IT, for example for typing, electronic mail, diary management, and are expected to do most of this type of work themselves. As one respondent put it:

> *'Managers are increasingly being expected to stand on their own two feet and do more of this type of work themselves.'*

There was a widespread expectation that managers and professional staff would do most of their own typing (only more senior and/or older managers were excused!), with some organisations reporting that managers are now probably doing

90 per cent of it. However, some employers are monitoring more closely the amount of typing managers do, as it is considered inefficient for managers to spend too much of their time on this type of work.

While IT has reduced the amount of typing secretaries do, as discussed later on, expectations about the quality and accuracy of the work produced have increased considerably.

4.2.2 Structural changes

Our findings show that changes in organisational structures can also have a considerable influence in broadening secretarial roles and work content. In flatter organisational structures more senior secretaries are beginning to take over some of middle managers' responsibilities. These might include general office management, project work, functional tasks, as well as involvement in the recruitment, development, training and supervision of junior secretarial staff. At the top of the secretarial scale, PAs are often seen as their boss's 'right hand', and expected to run the office in their absence.

Much streamlining has taken place in most of the organisations included in the study; this has affected secretaries like all other occupational groups (and in a few cases more than others). The combination of the reduction in the number of secretaries and/or the expansion of their roles and responsibilities has led to a considerable intensification of work. Our findings are confirmed by a recent survey by the Industrial Society, which found that 90 per cent of organisations included in the study reported an increase in the volume of work undertaken by secretaries (Mair and Povall, 1995). The intensification of secretarial work and the additional responsibilities mean that the secretarial role is increasingly less likely to be a nine to five job, particularly at more senior levels.

4.2.3 Changes in organisational culture and working practices

Finally, we found that current trends in the field of management and organisation, ideas about total quality management, the notion of the learning organisation, and a commitment to encourage employees to develop their potential, has contributed to challenge traditional attitudes and perceptions about the roles of secretaries (among other groups of staff). The need to utilise staff more efficiently, coupled with these 'cultural changes', are leading to a considerable transformation in the secretarial role and place within the organisation, namely the shift from working only or primarily for one boss, to providing support for a team of people.

As noted in Chapter 3, while there will always be the need for personal assistants who provide support services to more senior managers (managing directors, chief executives, *etc.*), this group is becoming ever smaller. For example, in a government department of 2,000 employees, it was estimated that only five traditional PA type of positions will be needed in the future. An increasing number of secretaries in our sample organisations are assuming a crucial role within a team, as one respondent put it:

> *'Secretaries should increasingly act as a unit in the team, pulling the team together and acting as cogs that keep the wheel turning.'*

The shift from 'personal' to 'team' secretaries has been noticed elsewhere, and this was already apparent in the early 1990s (*eg* Skills and Enterprise Briefing, 1992). More recently the Industrial Society's study mentioned above found that 60 per cent of their sample organisations reported an increase in the ratio of managers to secretaries in the previous three years. In addition, 35 per cent of respondents anticipated that the ratio would increase further over the next three years (Mair and Povall, 1995). The shift from the one-to-one secretary to team player can greatly contribute to increase secretaries' visibility, and the visibility of their contribution and potentials. As Fitzsimons argues:

> *'Secretaries used to be part of the office furniture, seen but rarely heard . . . . A good secretary was an unremarkable one, efficiently obeying orders, and then returning mouse-like to her station behind the typewriter . . . . In the past it was quite traditional within a workplace to refer to "the secretary" as an almost dehumanised individual who should be seen but not heard . . . . Now they [secretaries] are becoming a key part of the team . . . the organisation skills a secretary needs have changed. With lots of people competing for a secretary's time, he or she will need to exercise assertiveness and understand the dynamics of organising the workload of a group.'* (Fitzsimons, 1994, p.28)

It clearly emerged from our research that the shift to team player, and from a passive to a much more active role, requires a secretary to have rather different skills which are discussed in detail below.

Finally, with employers focusing increasingly on the concept of organisational culture, and on employees' understanding of and commitment to their mission statements, we found that secretaries are increasingly expected to have an understanding and awareness of the business, of an organisation's operations and strategy, and an ability to apply this knowledge in the workplace. The changes some organisations are going through are increasingly involving all employees, including secretaries.

4.3 Traditional and current secretarial skills

Despite the emergence of new secretarial roles and functions, our research findings show that the traditional 'supporter' role is still predominant. In line with previous studies (*eg* Truss, 1993; Silverstone, 1984; Vinnicombe, 1980), we found that the main components of secretarial work include:

- gatekeeping
- routine office work
- text production.

In this section we explore traditional and current skill requirements under these three headings, while in the next section we look at the implications of the emergence of new secretarial roles and functions for skill requirements in the occupation.

4.3.1 Gatekeeping

Traditionally, secretaries, particularly those at more senior levels (*eg* executive secretaries, PAs), have had an important role as gatekeepers, and this was confirmed by our research findings. The extent to which secretaries are expected to use their judgement in dealing with in-coming information, prioritising and deciding who should deal with it, depended very much on the level of seniority. Similarly, the range of people and the type of information a secretary is expected to deal with, depended on seniority. However, we found that apart from more junior secretarial staff who are expected to perform only the more routine clerical and secretarial tasks (*eg* typing, filing, photo-copying, *etc.*), the overwhelming majority of secretaries would act as gatekeepers and information handlers to a greater or lesser extent. This can vary from opening the post and screening phone calls to, for example, liaising with clients about contracts. As one respondent explained:

> *'While secretaries do not actually do the deal, they are expected to prepare the groundwork.'*

Our findings show that in order to fulfil this role, secretaries are normally expected to have a range of 'social and behavioural' skills and attributes. These include:

- oral and written communication skills
- inter-personal skills
- knowledge of the organisational structure
- understanding of the nature of the business
- familiarity with the technical, commercial and financial termin-ology.

Secretaries, particularly those at the higher level, are expected to be very good communicators, both orally and in writing, and have good presentation skills and telephone techniques. They need good personal skills such as tact, diplomacy, ability to persuade, and to give advice and feedback. If they are expected to liaise with other staff at different hierarchical levels, and in different departments, they also need to have a good knowledge of the organisational structure. As secretaries are increasingly expected to liaise with clients, they need a good understanding of the nature of the business. Secretaries working in a very specialised area also need to be familiar with the technical, commercial and financial terminology in use. We found that in the public sector, particularly within social and health services, and education, personal skills could be very important, as secretaries might be dealing with 'difficult', distressed and in some cases even violent service users.

4.3.2 Routine office work

The ability to use basic office equipment and technology (*eg* telephone, facsimile, photocopiers, filing systems, *etc.*) has always been a basic requirement for secretaries. But again our findings show that this function is expanding, with secretaries increasingly expected to manage and organise the office environment. Their tasks range from ensuring that there is an adequate supply of stationery, to researching and adopting new office procedures, and designing filing and library systems.

We also found that time management and prioritising of tasks are becoming essential and increasingly complex requirements for most secretaries. PAs to senior managers often have to make very complex arrangements at times, involving international travel, often at short notice. Similarly, team secretaries have to co-ordinate staff movements, arrange internal and external meetings, make travel arrangements, and take decisions about the priority given to different meetings and engagements. These tasks require secretaries to have excellent co-ordination skills, a good knowledge and understanding of the manager's and/or the team's work, and of key contacts outside as well as inside the organisation. When it is also considered that these functions are often undertaken in short spaces of time, and for high status people, the complexities and significance of this role can be more fully comprehended.

4.3.3 Text production

While traditionally this aspect of secretarial work has been limited to typing and maybe basic word processing, in the past decade, advances in IT and widespread computerisation have greatly expanded this area of work. We found that computer literacy and basic IT skills have become an almost universal requirement, and secretaries are increasingly expected to be familiar with a range of computer packages.

As discussed earlier, IT has reduced the amount of typing secretaries do. However, expectations about the quality and accuracy of the work produced has increased considerably. In most sample organisations, secretaries are expected to be able to do complicated word processing, spreadsheets and desktop publishing, and produce high quality documents ready for presentation or even publication. Traditionally, most of these tasks would have been sent to external specialised publishers.

The extent to which the widespread use of IT has meant that more traditional secretarial skills such as typing, audio and shorthand have become less important, is a matter for debate among professional organisations and other key players in this field. Views seem to be polarised between those who believe that traditional secretarial skills are destined to decline in importance, and those who argue that these will remain an essential part of secretarial work. The recently developed occupational standards (Business Administration NVQs/SVQs) are very general, and include the traditional secretarial skills mentioned above (*ie* motor skills) only as optional units, and only at levels two and three. This approach partly reflects the belief that the changing secretarial role, and the blurring of boundaries between secretarial and administrative functions, require more broadly based qualifications, which will increase flexibility and transferability both within and between occupations.

On the other hand, others believe that the lack of a specific focus on motor skills in the occupational standards has greatly diminished people's perception of the secretarial role, and fails to recognise the need to develop these skills, which are still demanded by employers. According to this viewpoint, there must be a recognition that secretaries can only learn to apply, use and develop these skills in a more complex, deeper, 'cognitive' and versatile way, once they have used them for a long period of time. Once secretaries have learnt to type and do shorthand, they must then develop their competency through speed and accuracy, for example. Many supporters of this view believe a separate series of occupational standards should be developed just for secretaries, to resolve some of these problems.

Differences of opinion on the emphasis one should place on motor skills are perhaps most evident in the 'accuracy versus time' debate, with some arguing that time in the traditional form of words per minute is one of the most important secretarial skills. However, others believe that accuracy and the overall outcome of a particular project are now more important and should take precedence.

The evidence from the interviews with employers presents a mixed picture. There can be no doubt that expectations about the level of accuracy have increased considerably. However, while employers still specify words per minute in their job descriptions, often this requirement is used as an easy and quick way of selecting candidates. With the exception of secretaries at more junior levels who might be spending most of their time copy typing, speed of typing does not seem to be very important to the type of work most secretaries do. It is generally more important that the work is completed accurately, within a specified deadline.

There also seemed to be a consensus that shorthand and audio typing are not so important anymore, with the former perhaps being regarded as having declined in importance more than the latter. As one respondent explained:

> *'Audio and shorthand are still an advantage, but are no longer hugely important.'*

Generally speaking, we found that audio typing and shorthand are unlikely to be 'standard' requirements. These are only specified if and when there is a need for them, as much depend on the individual working preferences of managers, or whether it is a function of their working practices. For example, only a few of the older and more traditional managers dictate letters to their secretaries. Dictaphones tend to be used by managers who are often out of the office and have to tape record letters and other information while they are 'on the move'. Such managers are often reported to have less time to devote to lengthy face-to-face dictation, which is increasingly seen to be an inefficient use of time. Minute-taking is still a common requirement. However, very rarely would one expect a verbatim account, and shorthand is therefore not regarded as essential for this task. Indeed, in some 'action' meetings a few 'flagged-up' bullet points are seen as sufficient record, and these are often taken down by managers.

4.4 New and future secretarial skills

Given the extent to which the occupation is changing, it was not surprising to find that secretaries are increasingly expected to have and to acquire new skills. These are closely linked to the emergence of new secretarial roles. The two most common 'new' roles emerging from our research include:

- team worker who provides support to a team of people and is perceived as a key link between team members
- independent worker who has her/his own area of work and responsibilities.

As mentioned earlier, the traditional 'supporter' role is still pre-dominant. However, we found that in some organisations the team player and/or independent worker roles are becoming increasingly important. These different roles tend to overlap, with some traditional secretarial tasks performed alongside new ones.

In this section we explore how new roles and functions are affecting the nature of secretarial work, and current and future skill requirements in the occupation.

4.4.1 Team worker

As discussed earlier, we found that in the sample organisations there has been a move away from the 'personal secretary' and towards the team secretary. This shift has implications for the type of skills secretaries are expected to have. In particular, their role as co-ordinators is becoming increasingly important. As the respondent quoted earlier explained, team secretaries need to act as 'cogs that keep the wheel turning'. They can provide an important link between team members, and between the team manager and other staff. They are increasingly expected to communicate with and provide information to other parts of the organisation, and to the external world, on the team's behalf.

As discussed later (Chapter 6), the transition from one-to-one to team secretary is not always an easy one, particularly as secretaries might find themselves with conflicting demands from different team members, and an increased workload. Our research shows that this new role requires secretaries to have additional skills. For example, managing pressure and conflicting demands, and assertiveness are requirements increasingly likely to be found in job descriptions. Teamwork is obviously becoming another essential skill. At the very least, a team secretary is expected to be able to work co-operatively with others and be willing to share ideas and information. In addition, some secretaries at more senior levels are also expected to be able to manage consensus and conflict, to motivate others, to recognise others' contributions and strengths, and to provide advice and feedback with diplomacy and tact.

4.4.2 The independent worker

Our findings show that some secretaries are increasingly taking responsibility for projects and areas of work not directly related to the work of their manager, or the group of people they support. We found examples of secretaries taking over specific projects, and these are discussed below. We identified two distinct areas where secretaries are more likely to maximise their opportunities for 'independent work'. These include IT and the broader area of secretarial training, development and supervision. These are outlined in more detail below.

Working on specific projects

Secretaries in some of our sample organisations are increasingly likely to take responsibility for specific projects. These can vary considerably, and here we can only give an idea of the most common examples emerging from the interviews. Arranging conferences is one area where secretaries are increasingly likely to get involved, and the extent of the involvement can be considerable, particularly if these are regular and/or large events. For example, secretaries might be expected to make decisions about the suitability and value for money of hotels and conference facilities. In some cases, they might attend conferences in the role of facilitators or administrators. Similarly, secretaries are expected to make travel arrangements, and take decisions about the most suitable and economical itineraries.

Other examples of secretaries taking over specific projects included the evaluation of new software packages, becoming responsible for the administration of the car fleet, co-ordinating office moves, developing IT and secretarial training packages, and investigating internal communication systems. There is also a belief among some employers that as secretaries are encouraged to develop their skills in areas of interest, they might get increasingly involved in functional areas of work (*eg* finance, personnel, PR and marketing) and eventually specialise and move into these occupations.

In terms of skill requirements, some have already been mentioned (*ie* co-ordination, organisation, communication). However, the variety of different projects a secretary might get involved with meant that they are required to have a wide range of skills, and above all they increasingly need to be flexible and adaptable. We found that attributes such as: problem solving, numeracy, bias for action, analytical skills, ability to influence, and net-working skills, sense of humour, sociable, friendly, initiative, self-reliance and resilience, are all increasingly likely to appear in job descriptions.

The 'IT expert'

As discussed earlier, secretaries in our sample organisations are normally expected to be familiar with a range of computer applications. However, our findings also suggest that they are increasingly expected to become 'experts' in some computer graphics applications. These include desktop publishing, word-processing, packages, spreadsheets and databases. This expertise is not simply used for 'traditional' secretarial tasks, but can give secretaries the opportunity to get involved in other areas of work as well. We found a number of examples which clearly illustrate how IT can contribute to secretaries' expansion into new areas of work. Firstly, secretaries' increased IT expertise means that in some cases they are expected to contribute to the organisation's IT policy. Secondly, secretaries' considerable experience of a number of computer applications, means that in many organisations they are assuming an important role as IT trainers and internal 'IT help desks', assisting managers, professionals and other secretarial staff.

Involvement in the development of the IT organisational policy and training are the two more common examples, and in future, secretaries' involvement with these areas is likely to increase even further. However, we found other examples of areas of work that secretaries are getting involved with through their IT expertise. These include: finance and budgeting; compiling statistical information; secondary research involving searching and retrieving information using on-line systems.

Secretarial training, development and supervision

While in the past some more senior secretaries might have had some responsibility for training and supervising more junior secretarial staff, on the whole these were not regarded as 'traditional' secretarial tasks, even at senior levels. However, we found evidence that this area of work is becoming more important due to a combination of factors.

First, as discussed earlier, secretaries' experience of a number of computer applications has meant that in many organisations they have assumed an important role as IT trainers. Our findings show that this role could be formally recognised, and secretarial staff might be allocated time to organise IT courses for other staff, and provide on-going support (*eg* providing a computer help desk). Even in organisations where this role is not formally recognised, secretaries are increasingly used by their colleagues for IT advice and 'on-the-job' training, as they are often the first to become familiar with new computer packages.

There also seems to be a trend towards secretaries playing an active role in the recruitment, supervision and development of more junior secretarial staff. We found examples of senior secretaries being involved in secretarial recruitment. In some organisations, more senior secretaries are expected to coach more junior staff, act as mentors, and advise managers on development and training needs. Again this role is formally recognised in some cases (*eg* through promotion, or pay bonuses), with secretaries running courses for more junior staff and being included in the recruitment process.

Our findings show that the skills required for this new role are again varied, and in more senior positions a high level of competency is expected. Secretaries involved in the recruitment process need to have interviewing skills, and in some cases they are trained to conduct aptitude tests. The type and level of skills depend on the extent of their involvement with this area of work. As a minimum requirement, secretaries fulfilling these tasks are expected to have an understanding of the organisation's approach to training and development, and have basic coaching skills. At the most extreme, at a more senior level, they have to be able to create a learning environment, to identify training and development needs, and develop appropriate training and development plans.

4.5 Conclusion

Table 4.1 summarises our main findings in relation to the changing nature of the secretarial role, and current and future skill requirements. It is important to stress the variability in the emergence and establishment of these trends in the different organisations included in this investigation. There is a widespread recognition that secretaries' roles and the skills they are expected to have are changing, and will change even further, in response to business needs and rapid organisational change. However, as discussed earlier, we found considerable differences between employers in terms of how far they had gone in restructuring the occupation and its role within the organisation.

Table 4.1: Old and new secretarial roles and skills

Role	Nature of work	Skill requirements
Support worker	*Role limited to gatekeeping information and providing administrative back-up*	— Oral and written communication skills
		— Inter-personal skills *eg* tact, diplomacy, ability to persuade
		— Knowledge of the organisational structure and nature of the business
		— Familiarity with technical and commercial terminology
		— Typing, audio and shorthand
		— Familiarity with a range of computer applications
		— Ability to collate, organise and edit information
		— Ability to use office equipment and technology
		— Ability to organise and manage the office environment
Team worker	*Provides support to a team of people and a key link between team members*	— Ability to manage pressure and conflicting demands
		— Assertiveness
		— Understanding of group dynamics
		— Ability to share ideas, provide information and feedback
		— Ability to manage consensus and conflict
		— Ability to co-operate and collaborate
Independent worker	*Has her/his own area of work and responsibilities, most common at the moment IT, and secretarial training, development and supervision*	— Ability to contribute to the organisation's IT policy
		— Ability to provide IT training and act as 'IT help desks'
		— Coaching and mentoring of junior secretarial staff
		— Supervision of junior secretarial staff
		— Interviewing skills

Source: IES Secretarial Study, 1996

The extent of variation means that any categorisation would tend to simplify a very complex and fluid situation, and the interplay of factors influencing it. Rather than attempting to categorise organisations according to their attitudes towards secretaries, it is more useful to think of a continuum. At one extreme, one would find organisations where secretaries still have a very traditional and narrow role: they are little more than 'office wives', they are expected to 'stick to the typing and coffee', and there are no immediate plans to review their position. At the other extreme, one would find organisations where secretarial roles and functions have been radically reviewed and redefined. In these cases, the secretarial role has expanded and developed to take on a wider range of administrative, IT, functional, project and junior management activities, to varying degrees. For example, in one company, competences for secretarial staff are modelled on the competences developed for managers. Most of the organisations included in the study can be found at various points along this continuum, often having come to terms with the need to review the position of secretaries, having developed or being in the process of developing a framework within which these changes can occur, but often finding that putting the theory into practice could be a very slow process.

5. Secretarial Recruitment and Skills Gaps

5.1 Introduction

As we have seen in the previous chapters, in the past few years, the secretarial occupation has been going through considerable change, and our findings point to a continued evolution and development of the profession in the near future. However, despite current and predicted changes, there was very little evidence from our study that employers have changed the way they identify the skills secretaries are expected to have. Indeed, while we found that employers are increasingly looking for a wider range and higher level of skills, on the whole they do not seem to have changed the indicators (*eg* educational qualifications), nor the recruitment methods they use to identify people with these skills.

This chapter explores and develops these issues in more detail, within a broader examination of the various ways sample organisations identify and measure the skills required for secretarial work. In the latter part of the chapter, we present some of the findings on current and future skill gaps, particularly in view of the extent to which the secretarial role seems to be expanding.

5.2 Secretarial recruitment

5.2.1 The process

As mentioned in earlier chapters, most organisations included in the study had reduced the size of their workforce in recent years, and on the whole secretarial recruitment (like that of most other occupations) had been rather low.

The two most common ways of recruiting secretarial staff seem to be via internal appointments and secretarial agencies. Most organisations have a policy of advertising vacancies internally first, to minimise costs and to give existing employees some career development opportunities. It is seen as particularly important to give secretaries this chance, as their career prospects are very restricted, given the short secretarial career structures, and the limited number of positions available at the more senior levels. Agencies are frequently used for temporary staff who are often offered a position permanently if there are no (suitable) internal candidates. This seems to be common practice in many organisations, which means that many secretarial recruits are assessed 'on the job', in addition to (or instead of) going through the usual selection process.

The vagueness of secretarial job descriptions (discussed in the previous chapter) is reflected in the indicators employers use to identify people with the right type and level of secretarial skills. This is particularly true of educational and vocational qualifications, but to a lesser extent it also applies to the type and length of previous relevant experience.

5.2.2 Identifiers

Generally speaking, the level of academic and vocational qualifications secretaries are expected to have tends to be very low. GCSE/'O' levels are not always expected. While secretarial qualifications (*eg* RSA, Pitman) are more likely to be an essential requirement, guidelines about expected types of qualifications and qualification levels (*eg* RSA I, II or III) tend to be rather vague and not clearly defined. As discussed later on, Business Administration NVQs/SVQs are not seen as very relevant by most employers. None of the organisations included in the study mentioned Business Administration NVQs/SVQs as a desirable or essential requirement for their secretarial posts, and many appeared to have a limited awareness of the qualifications. Our study seems to confirm what had been shown by the research findings discussed in Chapter 2 (*eg* Truss, 1993; Skill and Enterprise Briefing, 1992), namely that employers have little understanding of secretarial qualifications on offer, and tend to concentrate instead on typing skills.

There is very little evidence that in order to progress, secretaries need to have higher qualification levels, as discussed below. Suitability for more senior positions is judged almost entirely in terms of previous experience. Despite the guidelines issued by some professional organisations, there is also little evidence that typing or shorthand speeds are essential in appointing secretaries to more senior positions. Some managers are said to express a preference for shorthand or certain speeds; these are still required in some cases, but they are rarely used solely to screen people out. Having the 'right total' combination of skills is more important.

Discussions with professional secretarial organisations, anecdotal evidence from the media, and some research findings (*eg* Association of Graduate Recruiters, 1995) seem to suggest that in recent years there has been an influx in secretarial employment of progressively more qualified people (*eg* the widely publicised increase in graduates entering secretarial jobs). However, despite the availability of better qualified secretaries, generally speaking employers' expectations about the level and type of qualifications do not seem to have increased. Many respondents still regarded a secretary with a degree as being 'overqualified' for most positions, except perhaps for the more senior ones (*eg* PAs to more senior managers). Notable exceptions are organisations which have radically reviewed and redefined secretarial roles and functions. In these cases there is an expectation that younger recruits without considerable secretarial experience should have higher and broader qualifications. In addition, as the secretarial role is expected to develop further in these organisations, it is anticipated that in the future there will be an even greater emphasis on higher qualifications.

At present, however, previous relevant experience seems to be much more important than qualifications, although again guidelines about the relevant type and length of experience tend to be rather vague. Probably the most important way of assessing such experience was through references from past employers and, for internal candidates, recommendations from line managers. Sometimes appraisal assessments are also used for this purpose.

Generally speaking, employers seem to want people with some experience, even for more junior positions. Very few of the organisations included in the study recruited secretaries straight from college, as they need staff who are able to make a considerable contribution right from the start. This is clearly linked to the pressure to maximise efficiency, and to a decrease in the funding available for training and development. This was exemplified by the experience of one public sector organisation, which had to scrap a one year secretarial programme for school leavers because of funding cuts, in spite of the fact that this was regarded as an excellent scheme, which produced good people who progressed successfully through the organisation.

Considerable secretarial experience is always required for more senior positions (*eg* PAs, executive secretaries), but this can range from three to ten years. Often most of the experience is gained with the same organisation, but this requirement frequently seems to be because of the lack of mobility of older secretaries, rather than being something specifically required or expected by the employer.

The use of typing tests is still widespread, although some employers refrain from using them, and consider that lack of familiarity with a particular IT package warrants them unfair and less effective. In addition, candidates might be asked to take an aptitude or IT test. How the suitability of applicants is judged from the interview process varies considerably, sometimes with a lack of consistency even within the same organisation. Fairly sophisticated competency frameworks, clearly establishing what skills candidates need at what level, are the exception rather than the rule. More commonly, employers have a fairly simple list of desirable and essential skills and attributes, with little distinction between different types and levels of skills required for different secretarial positions.

5.3 Skills gaps

In discussing skills gaps both within an organisation and in the wider labour market, it is useful to distinguish two different kinds of shortages. The first includes shortages of 'traditional' secretarial skills, and is associated with the supporter role discussed earlier. The second is shortages of the 'new' skills which secretaries are increasingly likely to need as their role changes.

5.3.1 Traditional secretarial skills

In the current economic climate, the sheer volume of people applying for secretarial posts (like most other jobs) meant that most sample organisations had not encountered any serious difficulties in finding people suitably qualified and experienced. This may partly be a reflection of the fact that the study included a high proportion of large and prestigious employers, who tend to have less recruitment difficulties anyway.

Inadequate English language skills (*eg* grammar, spelling, punctuation) among younger secretaries were reported by some employers, although overall this does not seem to be a serious problem. Indeed, this is often partly compensated for by automatic spellcheck facilities within computer packages. In cases where shorthand is required, employers might find that many secretaries, even if qualified, tend to be a bit 'rusty', probably because nowadays most secretaries do not have the opportunity to use and practice this skill on a regular basis. But again this is not considered a serious problem, as this skill can be updated quickly and easily.

Internal gaps and mismatches in traditional skills do not seem to be widespread, and most employers seem satisfied with the type and level of skills of their secretarial staff. However, when these occur, they seemed more likely to be found in more 'traditional' organisations. Employers who have given little or no thought to ways of widening secretarial roles, who offer secretaries very little opportunity for development, and who tend to have low expectations from this group (partly reflected in rather low rates of pay) are those less likely to be satisfied with their secretaries' skills. In these cases, complaints about lack of specific skills are rare, and often the problem seems to be related to the overall quality of the secretarial group, as the quote below illustrates:

> 'The quality of some secretaries here is rather poor, they are slow, inefficient, bloody minded and not technically competent. Of course not all secretaries here are like that, but there are quite a few of them around, and you're bound to get them sooner or later.'

5.3.2 'New' secretarial skills

As is to be expected, gaps and mismatches in 'new' skills are closely linked to the changing secretarial role, and the new areas of work for secretaries. Often employers felt that the main problem is related to people's rigid and inflexible attitudes, rather than the lack of specific skills. Increasingly employers need secretaries to be flexible, adaptable, proactive and willing to exploit opportunities to broaden their own role. However, some reported considerable resistance to change amongst some secretaries, and an unwillingness to step out of rigidly defined occupational boundaries. The need for people with the 'right attitude' rather than with specific skills, is also related to the difficulty in anticipating future skill requirements in the occupation. Given that the potential opportunities for the expansion of secretarial roles are so numerous and varied, above all employers want their secretaries to be prepared to change.

The organisational and cultural factors which lead to this resistance to change are discussed in detail in the next chapter. In terms of the personal characteristics of secretaries who are more likely to resist change, these attitudes seem more likely to be found among those who have been in the profession for a long period of time, most of which has been spent in the same organisation. People who have entered the profession more recently seem to be much more willing to assume a less 'traditional' role. Indeed they can be very active 'agents of change', as they tend to have very different expectations compared with those who entered the profession in the past. As one respondent explained:

> *'Younger secretaries tend not to like the subservient role and are far less likely to be prepared to put up with the behaviour of some very difficult senior executives.'*

Clearly, secretaries who see themselves as being in partnership with their boss and/or team members are more highly motivated, and more willing to take on additional responsibilities. Above all, because they are not constrained by cultural stereotypes and narrow expectations, they are much more flexible and willing to respond to changing organisational needs.

Moving on to the specific skills gaps identified by employers, the most common ones include:

- **Time management and effective work planning.** Difficulties here are partly related to increased workloads, but also to the need to learn to respond effectively to the conflicting demands of different team members and learn to manage their expectations.

- **Team working.** Having traditionally been expected to work mainly or exclusively for one person, the transition to team player can be a difficult one, and some secretaries need to learn to understand group dynamics, to improve their communication skills, and to work co-operatively.

- **Assertiveness and confidence.** Given the traditional emphasis on the subservient role, some secretaries lack the confidence and assertiveness needed to take decisions, to be proactive and use their own initiative to deal with and influence a wide range of people inside, as well as outside the organisation.

- **Awareness of business/customer service approach and organisation's philosophy.** Given the marginal and often 'invisible' role secretaries have traditionally played, it is perhaps not surprising that some find it difficult to adjust to a situation where they are expected to have an active interest in the organisational and business strategies.

- **Awareness of some IT packages.** This is likely to be a problem where the packages are more advanced and require secretaries to undertake more sophisticated functions, such as graphics and statistical packages. Employers are generally trying to develop these skills through IT training. As younger secretaries become more exposed to such packages, in colleges and schools, this skill shortage is probably likely to diminish even further.

5.4 Conclusion

In conclusion, it must be emphasised that we found no evidence that there are currently serious skills shortages in the secretarial occupation. Our findings seem to confirm those of a recent Industrial Society survey. The authors found that the majority of employers interviewed (83 per cent) believed that most of their secretarial staff had the skills they currently need (Mair and Povall, 1995).

Any concerns about skill shortages are more likely to be related to future requirements. This is not surprising, given the extent of the expected changes in the future role and work of secretaries. Again, the Industrial Society's survey shows similar findings, with a considerable proportion of employers (37 per cent) believing that only a few of their secretaries have the skills the organisation is likely to need in the future.

In considering the findings on future skills shortages, it must be emphasised that some research participants believed that secretaries who enter the profession now seem better equipped to fulfil the 'new' role. Some believed that this is partly because secretarial colleges have identified and are trying to respond to employers' changing needs, and this is reflected in their course curricula.

Our findings also show that, despite the current and anticipated changes, there seems to be very little evidence that employers have changed the way they identify the skills secretaries are expected to have. Undoubtedly, more clarity about skills requirements, and more systematic ways of assessing secretarial competences, are essential in order to avoid a skills mismatch in the future.

6. Secretaries: A Neglected Resource

6.1 Introduction

Numerous studies have shown that secretarial work is one of the most highly segregated occupations (*eg* Kanter, 1977; Truss, 1993). This segregation takes a number of different forms. Firstly, it is one of the most highly feminised occupations in Western industrialised nations, with predictable consequences in terms of pay and working conditions, status, degree of stereotyping, and associations with domesticity. Secondly, secretaries have traditionally been excluded from mainstream organisational hierarchies and have constituted an isolated group of support workers. Isolation and marginality have seriously limited secretaries' career prospects. Within the occupation, career and development opportunities are very limited, with very flat career structures and with career progression happening more by 'accident' than by 'design'. In addition, the traditional close relationship between secretaries and their bosses, has meant that their role and status have been defined mainly in terms of the role and status of their managers. This contingency status has meant that secretaries' progression within an organisation has traditionally depended mainly on the progression of the their boss.

Despite the current and predicted changes in the secretarial occupation discussed in the previous chapters, we found little evidence that career and development opportunities for secretaries are in practice improving significantly. There are some notable exceptions, where some thought has been given to providing better and more opportunities for development, and for lateral as well as vertical career moves. However, often these 'experiments' are at a very early stage, with little sign yet of significant change, and with still a considerable gap between theory and practice.

In this chapter we first explore the training and development opportunities within the organisations included in the study. We then discuss training issues at the macro level, and explore the influence of vocational and educational qualifications on the content of secretarial work. The second part of the chapter looks at secretarial career structures, and opportunities for career development in the sample organisations. In the conclusion we highlight the factors which are contributing to blocking secretaries' career and development opportunities, and the efforts to improve their position within organisations.

6.2 Training and development opportunities

On the whole our findings seem to show that, despite the expansion in secretarial roles and responsibilities, and the expectation that this trend is likely to continue, very little thought has been given to the training implications. As one respondent explained, there is an assumption that secretaries will learn 'by osmosis'. Generally speaking there seems to be very little training available for secretaries, and this tends to be *ad hoc* and rather narrow in terms of content and areas covered. This lack of training opportunities is partly linked to the persistence of narrow and stereotypical views about the work secretaries do, and the type of training regarded as relevant to this group. Thus courses offered for managers in, for example, time management and inter-personal skills are often not seen as relevant to secretaries, while in many cases they obviously should.

Our findings seem to confirm the conclusions of a study by the Industrial Society (1993), which found that despite organisations' commitment to skill development, secretaries are often 'at the back of the queue' when it comes to training and development. A later report by the Industrial Society also confirms their previous findings:

> 'Despite the current climate of National Training Targets, Investors in People, NVQs and other accredited qualifications, it seems that organisations' recognition of secretarial and administrative contribution is not matched by an investment in secretarial training and development. While many jobs have expanded to accommodate rapid organisational change, their training does not reflect their increased responsibility.' (Mair and Povall, 1995, p.4)

There also seem to be inconsistencies within organisations in terms of access to training opportunities. These might depend on a secretary's location within the organisation's structure (*eg* in a department with a large or small training budget), the secretary's own determination, or more crucially on the manager's attitude and 'good will'. Scope for development in general tends to depend largely on one's manager, and in particular on their effectiveness in managing their secretary, their understanding of secretarial work, their ability to delegate (as opposed to 'dump') part of their work, and their willingness to redraw occupational boundaries in order to give their secretary more development opportunities. As a secretary who took part in the study explained:

> '*Secretaries have little control over their professional development, opportunities for development depend very much on their managers' attitude. If they want to use you simply as a typist, they will!*'

The research findings also show that lack of training opportunities can be linked to gender discrimination. There is a belief that some managers assume that most secretaries will leave to have children, and use this an excuse not to invest time and money in secretarial training and development. While this does not seem to be a widespread problem, it nevertheless emerged as a factor which can limit access to training.

The extent to which training needs are systematically assessed varies considerably. At one extreme, a sample organisation had no training budget for secretaries and no formal system for assessing their performance, training and development needs. In this organisation, secretaries receive no training at all. Most organisations had some form of appraisal, but the extent to which this actually works and results in development and action plans varied considerably. There was the example of one organisation where some managers refused to appraise secretarial staff. In others it was felt that the system has become too informal (*eg* a chat with your manager) and does not result in any plan nor action. However, this was not the case in all organisations. In some cases the appraisal system is better developed and works more effectively, resulting in the assessment of development and training needs, and an individual development plan.

The Institute for Employment Studies

In most organisations, secretaries' training and development needs seem to be assessed on an individual basis, with no system for identifying the skill development needs of the group as a whole. An exception to this seems to be when new computer packages are introduced and most secretaries are expected to learn how to use them. There were a few organisations which were looking at training needs as part of the process of redefining the role of the occupation. For example, one organisation had commissioned a training needs analysis to map out the wider range of functions that secretaries might perform in the future, to align competences to these functions, and to identify the development and training required to achieve this transition. Similarly, there were moves in a few other organisations to adopt a more systematic approach to the assessment of training and development needs, based on expected competences for different positions, and in line with the organisation's business plan and mission statement.

Apart from IT training, there do not seem to be training areas or courses which are specific to this occupational group, and which are offered by most or all organisations. Some provided limited training in 'traditional' secretarial skills such as minute-taking, telephone techniques, shorthand. However, there were also examples of courses which reflected trends in changing secretarial roles and responsibilities. These included:

- assertiveness and confidence building

- personal effectiveness

- communication skills

- business awareness

- 'learning to manage your manager' and 'learning to manage your secretary' courses attended by both secretaries and their managers; these are aimed at improving working relationships by increasing awareness and understanding of the nature of secretarial work, and exploring ways in which occupational boundaries and responsibilities might be redrawn, and how secretaries can be used more effectively.

Apart from a few notable exceptions, NVQs are not seen as part of the secretarial development programme (if there is one!). This is normally either because the organisation has decided for various reasons not to use NVQs, because the Business Administration NVQs are not seen as very relevant to the work secretaries do, or because the organisation is not even familiar with the qualification. This seems to confirm the results of the recent Industrial Society study which found that only a very small proportion of secretaries in their sample organisations were working towards NVQs (Mair and Povall, 1995).

6.3 Educational qualifications and work content

In looking at the changing nature of secretarial work, it is important to consider the general influence of vocational training and educational qualifications on work content. Clearly secretarial roles and functions depend largely on employers' attitudes and human resource strategies, and secretarial qualifications will develop largely in response to employers' needs. However, those responsible for developing national occupational standards have a role in encouraging employers to think about the most efficient ways of utilising their secretarial staff.

Truss's (1993) comparative study of the secretarial occupation in England, Germany and France highlighted in Chapter 2, has shown an interesting relationship between training and work content. Truss found that in England, secretarial training has traditionally been narrow (*eg* mainly focused on typing, audio and shorthand), has taken place separately from general academic education, and has been administered by different accredited bodies. On the other hand, in Germany and France secretarial qualifications have traditionally extended beyond the pure boundaries of secretarial training, to include broader academic subjects. Truss's research established a correlation between type of training and work content. In England, the narrow focus of the training seemed to be reflected in the narrow range of tasks performed at work. English secretaries were much more likely than their French and German counterparts to be spending time on routine office work. Conversely, German and French secretaries were far more likely to work on non-traditional secretarial tasks.

As discussed earlier, with a few exceptions, employers' expectations about the type and level of qualifications secretaries are required to have are still rather low and have not been updated. The status of an occupation is clearly linked to entry requirements, including qualifications. The lower these are, the lower the status of the occupation is likely to be. As Steedman has argued:

'The "value" of an award is the sum of its position in the hierarchy of educational awards, combined with a demand factor from the labour market.' (Steedman quoted in Truss, 1993, p.567)

It seems that greater clarity and higher expectations about entry requirements could considerably improve the status of the occupation and the contribution secretaries can make.

NVQs could make a significant impact in this respect, firstly, because the work based learning approach can provide people who have much work experience with the opportunity to gain some qualifications. Secondly, the wide focus of these qualifications, and the emphasis on flexibility and transferability, seem to be in line with the new role secretaries will be asked to fulfil. However, the take-up of the Business Administration NVQs/SVQs seems to have been rather low (IES, 1993). Our findings and a recent Industrial Society study (Mair and Povall, 1995) seem to confirm this observation. Given the extensive consultation process and mapping exercise which preceded the development of the new occupational standards, this 'lack of interest' on the part of employers seems surprising. Some respondents in the exploratory interviews suggested low take-up may require a greater emphasis on 'selling' the occupational standards, and therefore may be due to a lack of awareness amongst employers. Others believed that it was in fact the emphasis on general administrative skills, rather than specific secretarial skills within the occupational standards, that was inhibiting take-up and giving rise to this lack of interest. Following this rationale, they felt employers are sceptical of the relevance and effectiveness of the occupational standards and Business Administration NVQs/SVQs.

Within the remit of the current study, we were unable to explore in detail the relevance and take up of NVQs/SVQs among secretaries, and our conclusions are very speculative. Indeed, this was not a main objective of the study. However, we feel that this issue, and the wider issue of the link between the 'new' secretarial roles and training merits further exploration.

6.4 Secretarial career structure

In line with other empirical research and observations in the literature (outlined earlier in Chapter 2), the typical career structures for secretarial staff, in the organisations studied, are quite short. These generally range from as few as only one or two levels or grades, to four or five levels at most. These secretarial levels commonly reflect the status and level of responsibility of the manager the secretaries serve, and their corresponding level of work. Thus senior managers with much responsibility and highly important and confidential work, would have a higher grade secretary working for them.

The most common career routes identified usually progress through a number of job titles.

- At lower levels are titles such as junior secretaries, technical assistants, typists, word processors and clerk/typists. These individuals typically have fairly narrow functions, deviating little from basic copy and audio typing, and general office skills such as filing and photocopying. In some cases the lowest grades are essentially just copy typists, who work within typing pools.

- At middle grades are job titles like secretaries, personal secretaries, departmental, section and divisional secretaries and secretary/administrators. These secretaries generally undertake a wider range of functions, including diary management, making travel arrangements, entertaining and such like.

- At senior levels are titles such as senior management secretaries, senior personal secretaries, director and board secretaries, executive secretaries and personal assistants. At the most senior levels, secretaries may undertake some junior managers' tasks such as budgeting work, staff supervision and project work as well as traditional secretarial functions.

There are exceptions to this so called 'typical' career structure. In one organisation, for example, an increasing number of secretaries of varying levels are no longer being differentiated by job title. As the secretaries' working practices are being re-organised, and an increasing number are re-allocated to serve teams or groups of managers, rather than one individual manager, differing levels of secretaries are being called the same thing: namely team administrators. Although the precise nature of these secretaries' jobs differ, as do their grades and levels of pay, the job title does not. In other cases, although secretaries of differing levels have different job titles, these are not widely used or referred to within the organisation, and it is more common to differentiate between different secretaries by their job grade, for instance grade A, B and C.

Sometimes the most senior secretaries, such as executive secretaries and PAs are, because of their seniority, outside the secretarial route altogether. These PAs are in a completely separate job structure, which is generally perceived to be more commensurate with their additional tasks and responsibilities. However, PAs do not normally follow a different career route, and in most cases they start their career as junior secretaries or even in the 'typing pool'.

6.5 Career development

The lack of career development opportunities in the secretarial occupation is well documented (*eg* Crompton and Jones, 1984; Truss, 1993), and this is closely linked to the segregated nature of the occupation which was discussed earlier. On the whole, our findings seem to confirm the belief that a secretarial career is almost a 'life sentence', as Grassl has argued:

> '*Once a secretary, always a secretary, even if she becomes a Director's PA: her efforts promote her boss's career more than her own.*' (Grassl, 1984, quoted in Truss, 1993, p.573)

Our findings show that in most organisations included in the study, secretaries' opportunities for career development are very limited. Even in organisations where secretarial roles and functions have been expanded, these are not normally reflected in better carer opportunities, or improved pay and working conditions.

As mentioned earlier, secretarial career structures in our sample organisations tend to be rather short, with very few positions available at the more senior levels. PAs and executive secretaries were described by one respondent as a 'small and largely static elite'. Indeed, turnover in general tended to be quite low, thereby creating few opportunities for secretaries to move at all within the occupation.

One of the key characteristics of secretarial career structures is that they tend to be shaped around the managers' hierarchy, with the secretaries' status and position being inextricably linked to those of their bosses. In virtually all organisations included in the study, the seniority of the secretaries depends on the seniority of the managers they work for. Despite the move to team secretaries, these are almost inevitably lower down the career and hierarchical structures, with the most senior and better rewarded positions reserved for PAs.

This contingency status often means that career development within an organisation is more about 'following your boss' and being in the right place at the right time, rather than being related to skills and abilities. As one respondent explained:

'Secretarial careers happen more by accident than by design, as there is no established career route.'

There were examples of secretaries being at different levels within the same organisation, simply because this reflected the position of their manager, but with little or no differences in terms of work content and the competences they were expected to have. As has been argued before (Truss, 1993) the secretarial hierarchy appears to be an artificial one, as it does not lead to authority nor responsibility, but simply to increased status.

Previous research has shown that secretaries have traditionally been excluded from internal labour markets, and have been described as 'organisational isolates' (Kanter, 1977). Our research findings also show that, within the sample organisations, opportunities for development outside the occupation are rare. Even movements into neighbouring occupations (*eg* administration) are not very common. There was one exception of a media company where secretarial positions are seen as a stepping stone into production, and with most secretaries eventually moving into this area of work. However, apart from this example, even in the few organisations where there have been some attempts to increase opportunities for intra-occupational mobility (*eg* into functional areas), very few secretaries seem to do so. While some organisations gave examples of secretaries who have moved into management or have had a successful professional career within the organisation, these seem to be very much the exceptions that confirmed the rule. This may reflect the fact that where these development schemes have been implemented, they are still very much in their infancy and are thus not fully appreciated or utilised by the staff. Conversely these schemes may have been less effective in practice. It was difficult to discern this with any real certainty at this stage.

6.6 Career 'brakes'

Our research findings indicate that traditional attitudes and stereotypes seem to limit secretaries' career opportunities. There is a strong pressure, particularly in more traditional organisations, to 'keep secretaries in their place' — *ie* sticking to the typing and coffee, and enhancing the status of their manager by virtue of their presence. Traditional and stereotypical attitudes also make it very difficult for secretaries to move to neighbouring occupations within the organisation. The respondent from a government department quoted below exemplifies the views expressed by other research participants:

> 'You have to be bloody good to become an executive officer if you are a secretary, because secretaries are secretaries and are not expected or seen as capable of progressing in career terms.'

The move into higher level jobs requires the acquisition of specific technical and functional skills, and higher qualification levels. These requirements raise questions about access and development opportunities for all low level occupational groups. However, in the case of secretaries, prejudices and stereotypical views are preventing the development of highly qualified secretarial staff (*eg* those with a degree). In addition, secretaries face considerable obstacles even if they want to move into neighbouring occupations where most their skills and expertise would be relevant.

Not only do these attitudes represent a serious obstacle to secretaries' career development, but they can also stand in the way of changes needed to allow organisations to make a more effective use of this occupational group. These views may not only be held by managers, but by secretaries themselves who are caught up in a more traditional culture where secretaries are less required to show initiative, and perhaps have been more used to being told what to do. As another respondent explained, these attitudes are held by people:

> ' . . . who do not want to step out of their comfortable existence, they are bosses who still see a secretary as a status symbol and secretaries who are not ambitious and career minded.'

We found that that in many cases the perception of secretaries as a status symbol can make the transition from the one-to-one to the team secretary rather difficult, for some managers having to share 'their secretary' has a deep symbolic meaning, namely it is seen as an attempt to diminish their power and status. Similarly, because traditionally a secretary's status and position has depended on the status and position of her/his manager, the move to a team can be considered a demotion. Seemingly because it blurs the line of responsibility to the manager, some secretaries are finding this transition very difficult. As one respondent explained:

> 'Some people are having problems adapting to new ideas, for example, some secretaries are upset to have to spend more time typing for other managers and have less time to devote to their "old" manager.'

Our research findings point to a combination of factors which impinge negatively on secretarial career and development opportunities. The same factors also prevent the transition to a system where secretarial support staff are allocated on the basis of demonstrated needs. The age of managers and secretarial staff was often mentioned. It is believed that people in the latter part of their career are more likely to hold traditional attitudes, although such attitudes can also be found among staff in mid career. The bureaucratic nature of the organisation can also act as an obstacle. Changes in general are more difficult to implement in these organisations, as traditional values and attitudes are more entrenched and difficult to challenge.

Our findings also show that the expansion of the secretarial role, and improvements in career opportunities, tend to involve the redrawing of occupational boundaries. This again can lead to resistance, as other occupational groups (*eg* junior and middle managers, administrators) might perceive this as a threat to their professional identity, and as an attempt to diminish their power. This seems particularly to be the case in very hierarchical organisations, where different occupational groups are very 'territorial' and have very rigid ideas about occupational boundaries. If this is combined with anxiety about job security, it can generate a great deal of resistance.

As mentioned earlier, most organisations do not seem to have an overall development and training plan for the occupation. Similarly, there does not normally seem to be a single person responsible for co-ordinating secretarial training and development. Often this responsibility is left to line managers, many of whom seem to have little understanding of the nature of secretarial work. In addition, they might not have organisationally established standards which enable them to judge secretaries' performance and identify areas for development and training. Moreover, as discussed earlier, even when criteria are established they tend to be rather vague and out of date.

Power relations were also identified as another obstacle to development. The gap between secretaries and managers (in terms of their respective hierarchical positions) means that some managers do not value or take into serious consideration their secretaries' views. On the other hand, and probably partly because of this attitude, secretaries might lack the confidence to discuss any problems and development needs with their managers. As one respondent put it:

> 'You've got a grade six (secretary) having to tell a grade one (manager) that they are not happy with the job; it's unlikely to happen.'

However, this is not always the case, and in some organisations the emphasis on assertiveness and 'learning to manage your manager' training provides partial evidence that this problem may be disappearing.

Finally, lack of time for training also emerged as another obstacle. This is partly related to the intensification of secretarial work discussed earlier. However, in some cases managers are very reluctant to release their secretaries to allow them to go on training courses. This is partly linked to some managers' failure to see the advantages of encouraging secretaries to expand their roles and responsibilities, and more generally their view that training and development are 'soft' areas. Since the benefits are not immediately apparent, they are often reluctant to invest time and energy in it. In addition, some managers' concern with their own workloads and meeting their own deadlines means that they impose their own needs first, before those of their secretaries.

7. Conclusion

7.1 Introduction

In this chapter we first present some examples of 'good practice' of organisations which are reviewing the roles of secretaries, and trying to find ways of giving them more development opportunities, in line with their business plans and human resources strategy. In the final section we use the available evidence to draw some conclusions on the future of the secretarial occupation.

7.2 Examples of good practice

Examples of good practice varied considerably in terms of the aims and objectives of the whole exercise, the means to achieve these, and the extent to which the theory had been put into practice. However, there was one common element to all these examples, namely a recognition that secretaries should be given more development opportunities, in order to increase their level of job satisfaction, their work motivation and career opportunities, and to respond to changing organisational and business needs. These programmes tended to have senior management support at the very least, and in some cases were actually initiated by senior managers. However, there were also examples where action was taken partly in response to pressure from secretaries themselves, who were very actively seeking change.

7.2.1 Satellites

In one organisation, the secretaries and PAs had recently been re-organised into 'satellites' including four to six secretarial staff, providing support to an average of five or six managers. These satellites included people with a mixed range of abilities and experiences, from staff who were previously working in the typing pool to PAs. These groups were largely self-managed (although at this initial stage they were receiving considerable external support), and were responsible for organising their own work and covering for colleagues' absences. At this stage the one-to-one relationship between PAs and their managers largely persisted. However, the intention was to move eventually to a system where support staff would develop specialist skills and be able to provide a high quality service, while at the same time maintaining job variety and involvement with a wide range of tasks.

Despite some initial resistance from most secretaries, after four months the scheme appeared to be very successful. The overwhelming majority of secretaries were now satisfied and committed to the scheme. The level of satisfaction had increased particularly among those who previously worked in the typing pool, and who now found that their job was much more varied and interesting. In addition, while the need to reduce costs was not one of the main reasons for the re-organisation, it was already obvious that some savings had been made, as both overtime and the use of agency staff had decreased considerably since the scheme was started. Alongside this re-organisation, they were also adopting a competency based approach to reviewing the whole range of secretarial activities. The aim was to link the competency framework with the organisation's business plan, and to develop clear career paths for secretarial staff.

7.2.2 A 'new' competency framework

There was another example of an organisation where the old view that secretaries should work for a manager and have a very limited range of tasks, was replaced with the idea of the team secretary. In this organisation, managers were now expected to do much of the more routine work that was previously done for them (*eg* most of the typing, using E-mail to communicate directly with colleagues), while secretaries were expected to become a crucial member of the team, and assume a much wider role. What was particularly interesting about this example was the extent to which the competency framework had been developed to reflect the role of the 'new secretary'. New secretarial competences, which had been modelled on those developed for managers, covered 15 areas and were rated on a scale of one to ten. It is not possible to review here all the areas covered by the framework and the different levels of competency expected. However, an example might give an idea of the extent to which the role of a secretary could develop within this organisation. In relation to the need to be able to work as part of a team, a secretary at the lower end of the scale was expected to have:

- an ability to work co-operatively with others and a willingness to share information and ideas.

At the highest level of the career structure a secretary is expected to:

- be able to identify and combine people with different talents and abilities to achieve the best outcomes, be able to manage conflict, spot and publicise the success of an individual or the team, be aware and able to use a range of team building processes to create an open and high performance team environment.

Not only was this framework meant to improve career opportunities within the occupation, but it was also aimed at encouraging lateral moves into functional and professional areas.

7.2.3 Empowering secretaries

The sample also included an organisation which had aims similar to those discussed above, but which placed the main emphasis on empowerment. This was the result of a wider programme of cultural change and restructuring, where devolved leadership and empowerment were meant to influence management practice and employees' performance. Secretaries were being empowered to do more and were getting involved in more project work, departmental functions and meetings, and they were exposed to a wider range of people both internal and external to the organisation. In addition, on an experimental basis, secretaries in two divisions had been encouraged to develop secretarial focus groups to give them the opportunity to discuss and evaluate their work, progress and problems. The overall aim of the group was to increase the quality and efficiency of working practices, and foster a 'bottom up' culture where secretaries could become 'active agents' of the change process. Within such a process secretaries were intended, through consultations with their manager, to identify their training needs and to assume a more proactive role in their own development.

7.2.4 Job and professional structures

Finally, an interesting example was provided by an organisation which had developed a professional growth structure, in addition to the more 'traditional' job structure. The former was meant to act as an additional incentive to personal development. The organisation had a substantive job structure with five secretarial grades which were established in relation to the grade and level of responsibility of the manager. The professional growth structure was intended to work alongside, and hence to complement, the substantive job structure, and provide development opportunities within the same position. Thus, a secretary working and remaining at a lower substantive job level could aim to work towards higher professional growth levels and, in so doing, could enhance her/his skill development and abilities, and achieve a higher salary whilst remaining in the same job.

In other words, an individual may have been promoted to the professional growth level of 'senior secretary', for instance, and undertake higher level activities and work, but still be working within a position which was established at the lower substantive job structure level of 'secretary'. Only the personal job title changed, not the substantive title. This meant that if the individual left the job, it would still be advertised as a secretary. Thus, the individual had developed and not the job.

Individuals who wished to advance through the professional growth structure had to apply in writing via their line manager and local personnel manager to a Secretarial Review Board. This Review Board attempted to evaluate an individual's performance against the specified criteria for the appropriate growth level, and by so doing judged whether they could proceed to a higher level. In this way the Review Board aimed to establish and maintain the standards of steps in professional growth of secretaries.

7.3 The future of the secretarial occupation: demise or metamorphosis?

A key issue that emerged from the exploratory interviews and which is also attracting some media attention (*eg* Coren, 1996) is whether the secretarial occupation is destined to disappear in the future. Some of the respondents who took part in the exploratory interviews, for example, could quote a number of companies which do not employ a single secretary any more. It is argued that the occupation has shrunk considerably in the past few years, and as most traditional secretarial functions disappear, or are taken over by other groups of staff, their numbers will decline even further. According to this point of view, in the future, the secretarial occupation will be reduced to a small number of people at the two extremes of the occupational structure, namely, word processor operators at one end, and PAs to a small number of most senior managers, at the other end of the spectrum. This may be partially supported by the statistical data presented in Chapter 2, demonstrating a decline in the secretarial and clerical occupations.

On the other hand, other interviewees argued that as the 'paperless office' will never exist, there will always be the need for staff to provide secretarial and clerical support, even if their roles will be considerably different in the future. Some believed that in order to respond to changing organisational needs, secretaries will need to be even more highly competent in some of the more technical skills, as well as having better presentation, inter-personal, communication and organisational skills. In other words, rather than disappearing, this will become an occupation with higher entry requirements.

In many ways the debate is mainly about the definition of what a secretary is, and the nature of her/his work. Our research clearly shows that secretaries are still needed. In most sample organisations, the occupation had not been affected more than other groups of staff by redundancy programmes. We did not find a single organisation where there were plans to eliminate secretarial and support functions entirely. However, as we discussed earlier, the role of the secretary is changing, and in some cases this was reflected in a change in the job title (*eg* team administrator).

The findings of a recent Industrial Society survey also show that while a large number of job titles are included in the secretarial structure, the most common title used is still that of secretary, or variations such as private secretary, personal secretary, group secretary, *etc*. The survey findings in relation to changes in the size of the occupation are more mixed; just under a third of organisations reported that over the last three years the number of secretarial staff had remained the same. A further 33 per cent reported an increase, and 40 per cent a decrease, although the latter was believed to be due mainly to the recession (Mair and Povall, 1995).

In conclusion, our evidence suggests that secretarial roles are broadening, and that this trend is likely to continue, although, as discussed earlier, there is still often a gap between theory and practice. The issue of whether the job title will disappear, be expanded, or remain the same seems to be mainly academic. What seems far more important is the extent to which organisations are able to utilise better this often vital, but largely 'invisible' group of employees.

References

Anderson A, Marshall V (1994), *Core Versus Occupation-specific Skills*, Report by the Host Consultancy

Association of Graduate Recruiters (1995), *Salaries and Vacancies Survey: Summer Update*

Coren G (1996), 'So it's all over for secretaries . . . ', *The Times*, 19 February

Callender C, Connor H, Anderson A, Spilsbury M, Strebler M (1993), *National and Scottish Vocational Qualifications: The Case Studies*, IMS Report for the Employment Department

Crompton R, Jones G (1984), *White Collar Proletariat: Deskilling and Gender in Clerical Work*, Macmillan, London

Fearfull A (1992), 'The introduction of information and office technologies: The great divide?', *Work, Employment and Society*, Vol. 6, No. 3, pp. 423-442, September

Fitzsimons C (1994), 'The invisible edge', *The Guardian*, 16 May

Gilligan, C (1995), *The Role of the Executive Secretary/PA*, Technical Communications

Glenn E, Feldberg R (1982), 'Degraded and Deskilled: The Proletarianization of Clerical Work', *Social Problems*, Vol. 25, October, pp. 52-64.

Incomes Data Services (1994), *Clerical Workers' Pay*, IDS Study 560

Industrial Society (1990), *Secretaries: Still a Wasted Asset?*, London

Industrial Society (1993), *Typecast*, London

Kanter R M (1977), *Men and Women of the Corporation*, Basic Books, New York

Labour Force Survey (1995), *March 1995 to May 1995*, OPCS, London

Lane C (1989), 'New Technology and Clerical Work' in Gallie D (ed.) *Employment in Britain*, Blackwell

Lowe G S (1987), *Women in the Administrative Revolution*, Polity Press

Mair M, Povall M (1995), *Secretaries . . . Onwards and Upwards: The Future Role of the Secretary*, a Report for the Industrial Society and the Secretarial Development Network, London

Morgall J (1986), 'New office technology' from *Waged Work: a Reader,* (ed.) Feminist Review, Virago

Pringle R (1993), 'Male Secretaries' in Williams C L (ed.*), Doing Women's Work*, Sage, London

Pringle R (1989), *Secretaries Talk: Sexuality, Power and Work*, Verso

Rolfe H (1990), 'In the name of progress? Skill and attitudes to towards technological change', *New Technology, Work and Employment*, Autumn, pp. 107-121

Saunders B (1995), 'The wages of syntax', *The Guardian*, 30 January

Silverstone R, Toweler R (1984), 'Secretaries at Work', *Ergonomics* No. 27, Vol. 5

Skills and Enterprise Briefing (1992), *Clerical and Secretarial skills: A Neglected Resource?*, Issue 33/92, November

Skills and Enterprise Network (1995), *Labour Market and Skill Trends 1995-96*, SEN

Sleigh J (1979), *The Manpower Implications of Microelectronics Technology*, Department of Employment, HMSO

Truss C J G (1993), 'The Secretarial Ghetto: Myth or reality? A study of secretarial work in England, France and Germany', *Work, Employment and Society*, Vol. 7, No. 4, pp. 561-584, December

Truss C (1994), 'The Secretary as Supporter, Team Worker and Independent: A Case for Societal Comparison', *Gender, Work and Organisation*, Vol. 1, No. 4, pp. 205-216, October

Vinnicombe S (1980), *Secretaries, Management and Organisations*, Heinemann, London

Virgo P (1979), *Cashing in on the Chip*, Conservative Political Centre, May

Webster J (1986), 'Word processing and the secretarial labour process', in Purcell K, *et al.* (eds), *The Changing Experience of Employment — Restructuring and Recession*, MacMillan